HOME BREW BEER

HOME BREW BEER

DK

LONDON NEW YORK MUNICH
MELBOURNE DELHI

DK UK
Senior Editor Bob Bridle
Senior Art Editor Heather Matthews
Managing Editor Dawn Henderson
Managing Art Editor Christine Keilty
Senior Jacket Creative Nicola Powling
Jacket Design Assistant Rosie Levine
Pre-Production Producer Sarah Isle
Senior Producers Jen Scothern,
Oliver Jeffreys
Art Director Peter Luff
Publisher Peggy Vance

DK INDIA
Editor Kokila Manchanda
Senior Art Editor Anchal Kaushal
Assistant Art Editor Tanya Mehrotra
Managing Editor Alicia Ingty
Managing Art Editor Navidita Thapa
Production Manager Pankaj Sharma
Pre-Production Manager Sunil Sharma
DTP Designers Umesh Singh Rawat,
Arvind Kumar

Photography Tony Briscoe and Ian O'Leary

First published in Great Britain in 2013 by
Dorling Kindersley Limited
80 Strand, London WC2R 0RL
Penguin Group (UK)

2 4 6 8 10 9 7 5 3
001 – 192997 – Sept/2013

Copyright © 2013 Dorling Kindersley Limited

A CIP catalogue record for this book is available
from the British Library.

ISBN 978-1-4093-3176-6

Colour reproduction by Altaimage Ltd

Printed and bound in China by South China

Discover more at
www.dk.com

Contents

Foreword

Without a doubt, brewing your own beer and enjoying the fruits of your labours is one of the most satisfying pastimes there is.

My own career in the brewing industry grew out of a strong interest in home brewing. As a young boy I was fascinated by everything related to beer and brewing – perhaps fuelled by stories of my grandfather (who I never met) who was the head brewer of a local brewery. On family car journeys I would keep a log of every pub we passed, noting down the breweries whose names adorned each pub sign. When I started brewing my own beer, I sought to recreate the beers produced by those breweries, honing my recipes to get as close to the originals as possible. With each brew, I learned new techniques and made subtle adjustments. I made mistakes, too – and certainly this book would have helped me avoid them – but even mistakes can have serendipitous results. The first golden beer I

brewed, for example, was the result of forgetting to add crystal malt to what should have been a darker ale.

I am as excited about brewing today as I was 33 years ago when I produced my first batch. As you prepare your own beer, whether using malt extract or more complex methods, you are bound to feel a similar sense of excitement, especially as the moment of truth arrives and – having waited patiently for it to ferment and condition – you can finally taste your brew.

Brewing your own beer at home is relatively simple and extremely rewarding. With a good cleanliness regime, careful control of temperature, and the freshest ingredients, you should be able to produce beer that is at least equal, if not superior, to anything produced by professional brewers. You may even decide to recreate abandoned beers and styles that may not have been produced commercially for generations. What is certain is that with so many hop varieties, malt variations, and yeast strains available, the possibilities for experimenting with different flavours are endless.

My career has always been driven by the simple joy of producing special, well-crafted beers. Whether you are brewing for your own consumption or are hoping to bask in the compliments of others, I hope this book will help you get as much enjoyment out of brewing as I do.

Forever thirsty,
Keith Bott

Chairman of the Society of Independent Brewers

Introduction

If you enjoy drinking beer, then home brewing is the perfect hobby. Not only will you have the sense of satisfaction that comes from producing your own great-tasting beer, but you will also be able to create any beer style you like – including those not readily available commercially.

FUN, FRUGAL, AND FRIENDLY

Home brewing is relatively easy and can work out at a fraction of the cost of buying beer in the shops. The chances are, of course, that you will want to reinvest any savings you make, perhaps by buying new equipment. Even so, you should still be able to break even, which is not a bad return for such an enjoyable and fulfilling hobby. As well as being cost effective, home brewing is a particularly unselfish interest, as there are always plenty of delicious samples to offer around. In fact, you will probably produce more beer than you can hope to drink – so the more the merrier!

HOME-BREW BASICS

Making beer from a kit is no more difficult than preparing a ready meal – and the results can be truly impressive. With the minimum of fuss you can make, ferment, and barrel a surprisingly good batch of beer. While many home brewers are content with this approach, if you are reading this book, you are probably seeking something more involved. You'll be happy to know that with just a little extra effort, the possibilities for producing professional and bespoke beers are almost endless.

MALT-EXTRACT BREWING

The next logical step up the home-brew ladder is to produce beer using malt extract. This is still a relatively straightforward process requiring minimal equipment, but one that allows you to experiment with a wider range of ingredients, all the time gaining in confidence. The satisfaction of following a recipe and creating a beer using raw ingredients adds so much to the final product. Using fresh hops, for example, makes a huge difference to the quality of the finished beer.

HONING YOUR SKILLS

Sooner or later, though, you will want to try your hand at the full-mash (or all-grain) method – the "holy grail" of home brewing. There is an art to full-mash brewing that takes more time, research and practice, and you should think of it as an ongoing quest. As you temper and hone your skills, however, the quality of your brews will continue to improve. Just as importantly, you will be able to produce consistently good results and be able to brew exactly the type of beer you had intended to make at the outset.

EXPLODING SOME MYTHS

You may have heard various home-brew horror stories involving exploding bottles and upset stomachs, or you may have been put off by a bad experience in the past. Exploding bottles are a possibility, of course, but an unlikely one if you follow the instructions carefully – and beer is unlikely to make you sick as the alcohol will kill off most forms of bacteria. Today, the quality and availability of home-brew ingredients is better than it has ever been, and there is a wealth of information, advice, and support available.

SOMETHING FOR EVERYONE

In this book I have tried to cover as much ground as possible without getting too caught up in the details. Whole books have been written about yeast, for example, or brewing one particular style of beer, but I believe it is far better to master the basic techniques and methods first, before specializing in any one area.

The recipes in this book cover every major style of beer, so you should be able to find the perfect lager, ale, wheat beer, or "mixed style" for you. Some recipes are more difficult to brew than others, but you should simply regard these as a challenge. As with all crafts, the more care and effort you put in, the better the results will be, so don't worry if you don't get it quite right every time – your beer will still taste good.

I hope you enjoy making these beers and that you find the recipes appealing and inspiring. Home brewing is one of the best hobbies around and I am sure you will enjoy it for many years to come – sandals and beard are optional!

Greg Hughes

Introduction

A brief history of brewing

Beer production has a long and fascinating history that can be traced back millennia – from the ancient plains of Mesopotamia to the current trend for home brewing worldwide.

7000BCE – Nomadic hunter-gatherers in Mesopotamia (present-day Iraq) **grow and harvest an ancient form of grain**, which is thought to have been used to make an early form of beer.

Pottery chips found in a Neolithic village at the Jiahu site in China contain **traces of compounds found in alcoholic drinks.**

1100–1200s – Commercial hop cultivation **begins** in northern Germany, followed by the export of hopped beer.

822CE – Abbot Adalhard from the Benedictine monastery at Corbie in northern France writes a series of statutes covering the running of the monastery, which includes gathering sufficient hops for making beer – **the first documented link between hops and brewing.**

Fresh hop cones

Barley grains

1516 – The Beer Purity Law or "Reinheitsgebot" is established in Bavaria. It states that barley, hops, and pure water are the only ingredients allowed in the brewing process. It doesn't extend to the rest of Germany until 1906.

1710 – The use of **bittering agents other than hops is banned** by Parliament in England to secure revenue for a hop tax. As a result, hops become the dominant bittering agent in beer throughout the western world.

7000BCE	4300BCE	822CE	1040	1100–1200s	1412	1516	1587	1710

4300BCE – Babylonian clay tablets dating from this period include details of a **recipe for an alcoholic drink made with grain.**

1412 – The earliest record of **hopped beer** being brewed in England.

"The brewer" – from a 16th-century woodcut

1040 – The first commercial brewery is founded in Weihenstephan Abbey, Bavaria, where the process of brewing becomes a commercial venture by the monks.

Across Europe throughout the Middle Ages, beer becomes one of the most popular drinks. As it is boiled prior to fermentation, it is a safe source of hydration at a time when most water sources are unclean. Its calorie content also makes it an important source of nutrition.

Hopped English ale

1587 – Colonist settlers in Virginia, North America **brew their first batches of beer** (although they still send back to England for more).

1810 – A festival to celebrate **the marriage of Crown Prince Ludwig** is held in Munich, Germany, which goes on to become the famous **Oktoberfest beer festival**.

Traditional German beer stein

Hop bines

1990s–PRESENT – The home brewing world starts to expand rapidly with a whole range of kits and ingredients coming onto the market.

Today there is a renewed surge of interest in home brewing, with UK-based manufacturers Muntons selling more than 500,000 kits in 2012, twice as many as in 2007.

Home brew kit

1950s – During the summer holidays in the UK, up to **10,000 people**, including whole streets of families, leave London for the hop fields of Kent to **pick hops for the local breweries**.

1857 – French chemist Louis Pasteur discovers that **yeast is responsible for alcoholic fermentation**. This advancement allows brewers to control fermentation, leading to better quality beers.

Dried brewer's yeast

1971 – English journalists Michael Hardman, Graham Lees, Bill Mellor, and Jim Makin discuss setting up a **consumer organization for beer drinkers**, which goes on to become the Campaign for Real Ale (CAMRA).

Pints of real ale

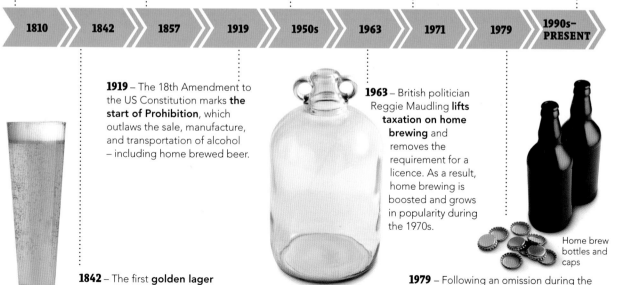

| 1810 | 1842 | 1857 | 1919 | 1950s | 1963 | 1971 | 1979 | 1990s–PRESENT |

1919 – The 18th Amendment to the US Constitution marks **the start of Prohibition**, which outlaws the sale, manufacture, and transportation of alcohol – including home brewed beer.

1963 – British politician Reggie Maudling **lifts taxation on home brewing** and removes the requirement for a licence. As a result, home brewing is boosted and grows in popularity during the 1970s.

Home brew bottles and caps

1842 – The first **golden lager is produced in Pilsen,** Bohemia. It is a popular style now brewed worldwide.

Glass of Pilsner

Glass home brewing fermenter

1979 – Following an omission during the lifting of Prohibition in the US in 1933, **home brewing is finally legalized** thanks to the Cranston Bill.

INTRODUCTION A BRIEF HISTORY OF BREWING

15

The craft-beer revolution

The global beer market may still be dominated by large breweries, but in recent years there has been a rise in the number of artisan breweries producing craft beers.

70
CRAFT BREWERIES
are located in Canada's Ontario province alone

100%
INCREASE
in craft-beer sales was recorded in Ontario, Canada, between 2007 and 2010

500,000
HOME-BREW KITS
were sold by Muntons in the UK in 2012

50
NEW MICROBREWERIES
open each year in the UK

1,000
BREWERIES
were operating in the UK in 2012 – a 70-year high

132
LITRES
(232 pints) of beer were consumed per capita in 2010 in the Czech Republic – home to the world's thirstiest beer drinkers

15%
RISE
in craft-beer production was recorded in the US in 2012 (compared with a 1% growth rate in the overall beer market)

97%
OF BREWERIES
were classified as craft breweries in the US in 2012

1 MILLION AMERICANS
brewed their own beer at home in 2012

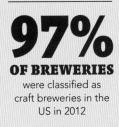

40
CRAFT BREWERIES
are located in Mexico, where craft-beer sales make up a small but rapidly expanding sector of the beer market

500%
INCREASE IN SALES
has been recorded at the Ilkley microbrewery in North Yorkshire since 2009

82
MILLION LITRES
(143.3 million pints) of beer were produced in 2011 by the association of French Craft Brewers

£323 BILLION

($495 billion) was the value of global beer sales in 2011; it is estimated that this will rise to £386.3 billion ($583.5 billion) by 2016

40%
OF BEER SALES WORLDWIDE could be accounted for by China by 2016

40.89 BILLION LITRES
(72 billion pints) of beer were consumed In China in 2010 – more than any other country

200 CRAFT BREWERIES
are currently operating in Japan

25% REVENUE GROWTH
was recorded at the Little Creatures craft brewery in Freemantle, Western Australia, during 2011

WHAT IS A CRAFT BEER?

A craft beer is any beer produced by a small, independent brewery using quality ingredients and traditional methods. Craft brewers specialize in attention to detail and produce beers often considered to be far superior to their mass-produced counterparts. While craft brewers do not have the big marketing budgets of the market leaders, they are freer to produce small batches of naturally carbonated, chemical-free beer – something the larger breweries would not find commercially viable.

From grain to glass

The brewing process involves steeping a starch – typically malted cereal grains – in water, adding hops for bitterness, flavour, and aroma, and then fermenting the resulting wort with yeast.

1. PREPARATION

Every piece of equipment that comes into contact with the beer must be thoroughly cleaned and sterilized (see pp46–47), as any stray bacteria will ruin the brew. Use sterilizing agents and a bottle-cleaning brush.

2. MASHING

The mash (see p59) is the process by which the starches in the malted grains are converted into fermentable sugars. The grains are steeped in hot (but not boiling) water to produce a sweet liquid called the wort.

BREWER'S YEAST +
MALT SUGAR =

C_2H_5OH
(alcohol)

CO_2
(carbon dioxide)

6. FERMENTING

The cooled wort is transferred to a fermenter and the yeast is pitched, or added (see pp62–63). The fermenter lid is closed, an airlock fitted, and the wort left to ferment at the specified temperature for about a week. During this time, the sugars in the wort are converted into alcohol.

7. PRIMING AND RACKING

Once fermentation is complete, priming sugar is added to condition the beer and add carbonation. The beer is then racked (transferred) to a storage container, such as a barrel or bottles, and left to condition.

3. SPARGING

The sparge (see p60) involves adding a fine spray of water to the surface of the grain to rinse out the fermentable sugars. The mash tun is drained and the sweet wort transferred to the boiler.

4. BOILING

The wort is then vigorously boiled (see p61) for an hour or more, and hops are added at various intervals. The boil sterilizes the wort and allows the hops to impart bitterness, flavour, and aroma.

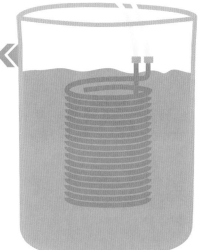

5. COOLING

After the boil, the wort must be cooled (see p61) to fermentation temperature (about 20°C/68°F) – if the wort is too hot, the yeast cells will be killed when it is added. A rapid cool reduces the chance of bacterial contamination and off-flavours in the beer.

8. CONDITIONING

Depending on the style of beer and the particular recipe, it will need to be left to condition for at least two weeks at the required temperature. This allows the beer to clear and lets the flavours mature.

9. SERVING

After conditioning, the beer is ready to be tasted. The priming sugar will add fizz, but if the brew is too flat, move it to a warm place for a few days and try again. If it is too lively, try chilling it before you pour.

Ingredients

Malt

This is cereal grain that has been allowed to germinate during a process known as malting. Malting creates enzymes that enable starches in the grain to be converted into fermentable sugars.

Barley is the most common grain used to produce malt for brewing. It is naturally high in enzymes and so has the potential to produce high quantities of fermentable sugar. Malted wheat and rye are also widely used in brewing.

There are three varieties of barley: two-row, four-row, and six-row, which refers to the arrangements of kernels around the grain shaft. Two-row barley is the most common variety used for brewing, as it is low in protein and produces more fermentable sugars.

THE MALTING PROCESS

Malt is produced in a building known as a maltings or malt house. Here, the grains are steeped in water, which causes them to absorb moisture and begin to sprout. When the rootlets have grown sufficiently, the grain is dried with warm air to halt any further growth. It is then "tumbled" to remove the rootlets.

Roasting the grains

Once the rootlets have been removed, the grains are roasted to create different types of malt – the higher the roasting temperature, the darker the malt and more intense the flavours. Lightly roasted malts have a high enzymatic (or diastatic) power and so produce lots of fermentable sugar when mixed with hot water during the mash (see p59). Highly roasted malts,

on the other hand, have less diastatic power and produce little or no fermentable sugar. These malts add colour, flavour, and aroma to a beer.

Floor malting

Traditionally, after steeping, the grains were spread out across the floor of the maltings to dry. There they were turned by hand using large rakes, which prevented mould from forming and ensured even drying. In the 1940s, industrial techniques were developed to improve the efficiency of the malting process, enabling the production of much larger batches of malt. Today, the traditional method is still considered to produce the best malts, although the practice is rare and malts produced in this way are generally too expensive for commercial breweries.

Crushing the grains

The malting process produces whole malt grains, which must be crushed before adding to the mash (crushing allows the enzymes to be converted into fermentable sugars efficiently). Most home-brew suppliers sell pre-crushed malts for convenience, but you can buy whole grains and crush them yourself if you prefer. The process can be messy and time consuming, but it will ensure that you are using the freshest grains. Once crushed, store them in an airtight container, where they will keep for a few months.

Whole malt grains

COLOUR RATING CHART

The colour of a malt – and the hue of a finished beer – is measured using one of three internationally recognised scales: the European Brewing Convention (EBC) – the scale used in the recipes in this book, the Standard Reference Method (SRM), and Degrees Lovibond (°L), the original scale developed by Joseph Williams Lovibond in 1883. SRM is approximately equal to °L; EBC is equal to SRM multiplied by 1.97.

COLOUR			
EBC	4	6	8
SRM/LOVIBOND	2	3	4
BEER STYLE	Light lager	Weissbier	Witbier

BASE MALTS

These are lightly roasted malts that make up the majority of the grain bill in a recipe and provide most of the fermentable sugars.

Pale base malts
Use Pilsner and lager base malts for very pale lagers and ales. For other ales and darker beers, use pale malts such as Maris Otter and Halcyon.

Darker-roasted base malts
Slightly darker roasted base malts, such as Munich and Vienna, will provide higher malt flavours, as well as lots of fermentable sugars.

Wheat malt
In addition to producing fermentable sugars, wheat also produces protein, which aids head retention and can add a hazy finish to the beer. Wheat can be difficult to use in the mash.

Rye malt
Less common than either barley or wheat malt, you can use rye to introduce spicy notes to a beer. Like wheat, it can be difficult to mash, so use only in small quantities.

Pale base malt

Wheat malt

SPECIALITY MALTS

These malts are all specially roasted for use in small quantities in the mash to add flavour, colour, and aroma. Unlike base malts, they contribute relatively few fermentable sugars.

Caramel malts
Also known as crystal malts, there are a range of caramel malts available, each heated to different temperatures. They introduce honey, caramel, and toffee flavours.

Amber malt
A type of roasted malt with a light, dry, biscuity flavour, amber malt adds a dark amber colour to ales and porters. Use only in small quantities.

Roasted malts
Darker-roasted malts have little or no fermentable sugar but provide complex colours, flavours, and aromas.

Caramel malt

Amber malt

Roasted malt

12	16	20	26	33	39	47	57	69	79	138
6	8	10	13	17	20	24	29	35	40	70
Belgian blonde ale	Honey ale	Pale ale		Mild			Black lager		Coffee stout	Imperial stout

Adjuncts and sugars

For some beer styles, you will need to use grains other than malted barley (see pp22–23), as well as additional fermentable sugars. These adjuncts and sugars all impart particular flavour characteristics.

TORRIFIED WHEAT
This is unmalted wheat that is gently cooked, then rolled to form a flaked grain. It adds a distinctive wheat flavour and increases the head retention of a beer.

SPELT
A close relative of wheat, spelt is a malted grain that imparts a delightful aroma and flavour. Use in small quantities as it can be overpowering.

FLAKED RICE
A common and cost-effective adjunct in American- and Japanese-style light lagers, flaked rice produces particularly crisp and dry beers with minimal flavour.

ROASTED BARLEY
This is a very dark unmalted grain similar to black malt (see p23), but with a less astringent bitterness. It introduces coffee notes that are ideal for stouts and porters.

FLAKED OATS
Easier to use than whole or rolled oats as they don't need to be cooked beforehand, flaked oats add a smooth, silky creaminess. Use in stouts and porters.

FLAKED MAIZE
Also known as flaked corn, this is one of the most commonly used adjuncts. It produces very light beers with a subtle corn-like character and neutral aftertaste.

MALT EXTRACT

This is the fermentable sugar from malted barley (see pp22–23) in concentrated form. Once re-hydrated, it can be boiled with hops to create a fermentable wort, or used in the same way as sugar to increase the original gravity, and for use in priming (see p66).

Malt extract is prone to oxidizing when exposed to air or moisture for extended periods so it is crucial that you use very fresh malt extract. Once opened, store in an airtight container in the fridge to keep it dry and slow the effects of ageing.

Dried malt extract

Dried malt extract (DME)

A fine powder also known as spraymalt, DME is produced by heating sweet wort and spraying it inside a tall, heated unit. The droplets dry and quickly cool causing them to solidify and drop to the floor where they can be collected. To use DME, reydrate it in a little cold water and then boil with hops to create a fermentable wort.

Liquid malt extract (LME)

This treacle-like substance is produced by heating sweet wort to evaporate some, but not all, of the liquid. Heating darkens the malt slightly, and this darkening will continue when it is boiled during brewing. If substituting LME for DME in a recipe, you will need 1.2kg (2½lb) of liquid malt extract for every 1kg (2¼lb) of dried.

Liquid malt extract

CANDI SUGAR

Often used in Belgian beers to increase the alcohol content without adding body, candi sugar is available in dark or light forms and adds depth of flavour.

HONEY

Most of the sugars in honey are fermentable, producing a dry yet distinctive honey character. Honey contains wild bacteria, so add near the end of the boil to sterilize.

MOLASSES

Also known simply as treacle, this dark, liquid sugar adds a complex, rum-like flavour. Use only in small quantities to add depth of character in high-alcohol ales.

MALTS, ADJUNCTS, AND SUGARS – AT A GLANCE

Name	Type	Description	Colour (EBC)	Requires mashing?	Maximum usage
Acid malt	Malted grain	Lowers the mash pH of lagers; use in small quantities	3	✓	10%
Amber malt extract (dried and liquid)	Malt extract	Use in malt-extract recipes to add colour	30	✗	100%
Amber malt	Malted grain	Imparts a deep amber colour and biscuit flavours	65	✓	10%
Aromatic malt	Malted grain	Adds a rich malt character; similar to dark Munich malt	150	✓	10%
Barley hulls	Adjunct	Bulks up the mash and helps the run-off; provides no fermenatable sugars	N/A	✗	10%
Biscuit malt	Malted grain	Adds biscuit character and colour	50	✗	10%
Black malt	Malted grain	Adds flavour and colour to dark beers; adds colour to light beers	1,280	✗	10%
Bohemian Pilsner malt	Malted grain	Very light malt; requires multi-rest mashing (see p59)	2	✓	100%
Brown malt	Malted grain	Adds strong bread-like flavours; between amber and chocolate malt in colour	105	✓	10%
Candi sugar (light and dark)	Sugar	Increases fermentable sugar levels; adds colour and authentic flavours	N/A	✗	20%
Cara amber	Malted grain	Promotes a full body and adds a deep red colour to amber and dark beers	70	✗	20%
Cara hell malt	Malted grain	Accentuates the fullness of the flavour in special German beers	25	✗	15%
Caramunich	Malted grain	Enhances flavour and aroma in golden to brown lagers and ales	200	✗	15%
Cara red	Malted grain	Adds body and increases the malt aroma in many beer styles	50	✗	10%
Cara rye malt	Malted grain	Introduces rye flavours and a pleasing brown colour	150	✗	15%
Cara wheat malt	Malted grain	Promotes a full body, adds a wheat aroma, and enhances the colour	100	✗	15%
Carafa special malt	Malted grain	Adds colour and aroma to dark lagers; an alternative to black malt and roasted barley	800–1,500	✗	5%
Carapils	Malted grain	Very light crystal malt; adds body and malt flavour, without adding colour	5	✗	20%
Chocolate malt	Malted grain	Adds colour and aroma to dark beers; can also be used in pale ales	800	✗	10%
Corn sugar	Malted grain	Use to increase gravity without adding flavour or aroma	0	✗	5%
Crystal malt	Malted grain	Available in a range of colours; adds subtle caramel colours and flavours	60–400	✗	20%
Dark malt extract (dried and liquid)	Malt extract	Use to increase gravity and colour	40	✗	100%
Extra light dried malt extract	Malt extract	The lightest malt extract; use for very low-colour beers	5	✗	20%

Name	Type	Description	Colour (EBC)	Requires mashing?	Maximum usage
Flaked barley	Adjunct	Adds a grainy flavour and improves head retention in stouts and porters	4	✓	20%
Flaked maize (corn)	Adjunct	Increases fermentable sugar level, while adding very little flavour or colour	2	✓	40%
Flaked oats	Adjunct	Used in small quantities in oatmeal stouts	2	✓	10%
Flaked rice	Adjunct	Provides body without adding colour or flavour	2	✓	20%
Honey	Sugar	Adds a dry finish with a distinct honey character	2	✗	100%
Lager malt	Malted grain	A light coloured base malt used for very pale beers	4	✓	100%
Light malt extract (dried and liquid)	Malted grain	A light malt extract used to increase the gravity in most malt-extract recipes	10	✗	100%
Maple syrup	Sugar	Used to add a distinct, dry maple character	70	✗	10%
Melanoidin malt	Malted grain	Adds a full flavour and increases colour and malt character	40	✓	15%
Mild ale malt	Malted grain	Use in brown ales and milds to impart extra flavour	10	✓	100%
Munich malt	Malted grain	Similar to Vienna malt, but slightly more roasted; adds lots of malt character	20	✓	50%
Pale malt	Malted grain	A base malt used in the majority of ales	5	✓	100%
Peat-smoked malt	Malted grain	A heavily smoked malt	3	✓	20%
Pilsner malt	Malted grain	Similar to lager malt, but usually produced using two-row barley (see p22)	3	✓	100%
Roasted barley	Adjunct	Adds nutty, roasted flavours and a deep red-to-brown colour	1,000	✗	10%
Roasted wheat	Adjunct	Adds a deep brown colour to dark wheat beers	900	✓	10%
Rye malt	Malted grain	Use to add rye flavours and spicy notes	10	✓	50%
Smoked malt	Malted grain	Usually smoked over beech; adds a distinctive smoky aroma to smoked beers	18	✓	100%
Special B malt	Malted grain	Adds a deep caramel colour and flavour	250	✓	10%
Spelt malt	Malted grain	Imparts spelt aroma notes	5	✓	20%
Torrified wheat	Adjunct	Use in wheat beers, and to aid head retention and flavour in ales	4	✓	40%
Victory malt	Malted grain	Adds an orange colour and nutty flavours	50	✓	15%
Vienna malt	Malted grain	Use in light amber beers for colour and flavour	8	✓	50%
Wheat malt extract (dried and liquid)	Malt extract	Use in malt-extract wheat beers, and to aid head retention in other beer styles	16	✗	100%

Hops

Hops are the cone-shaped flowers of the female hop plant – a climbing bine related to hemp. They are dried and added to beer for bitterness, flavour, and aroma, and to protect it from bacteria.

Native to North America, Europe, and Asia, hops are first thought to have been used in beer production in the 11th century. They were used instead of bitter herbs – such as dandelion, marigold, and heather – as they produced beer that was less likely to spoil.

Today, due to extensive breeding programmes aimed at creating more productive and disease-resistant plants, more than 100 different varieties are grown around the world. The main growing regions are the US, New Zealand, the UK, Germany, the Czech Republic, China, Poland, and Australia.

GROWING AND HARVESTING
Hop plants, which grow best vertically, are trained to grow up stringed supports – they can reach heights of up to 6m (20ft). The string supports are lowered during harvesting, allowing the cones from the tallest bines to be removed easily. Smaller dwarf varieties are also propagated, although these need to be grown over a larger area to yield a comparable crop.

Traditionally, hops were harvested by hand. Due to the high numbers of people required at harvest time, hop-picking became something of a social event. In England, for example, whole families would travel from towns and cities to the hop-growing regions on specially chartered trains and buses, living in temporary huts and spending several weeks picking the hop harvest. Today, hops are picked and dried mechanically, although the hop harvest is still a time of excitement, with many breweries producing beers made using undried "green" hops to celebrate the new harvest.

Fresh hop cones

Hop bines are trained to grow vertically up stringed supports, which can be lowered during harvesting.

BITTERING AND AROMA HOPS

Hops are added at various intervals during the boil (see p61) to impart particular characteristics to the finished beer. Hops added at the start of the boil impart bitterness, which balances the alcohol flavours and adds smoothness to the beer. Hops added later in the boil – typically during the final 30 minutes – impart flavour and aroma. These tend to be added in several additions depending on the desired character.

Another way of importing aroma and flavour from hops is to use a traditional method known as first-wort hopping, in which hops are added to the run off from the mash (see p59) before the boil. The hops are steeped, which causes them to oxidize and allows some of the beta acids to dissolve into the wort rather than being driven off. In blind tests, beers produced using this method were found to have a smoother bitterness and aroma, so it's worth experimenting.

Historically, hops were categorized as either bittering hops or aroma hops. Today, however, increasing numbers of hop varieties are suitable for both bittering and aroma, and are known as dual-purpose hops.

ALPHA AND BETA ACIDS IN HOPS

Hop resins contain alpha and beta acids, which have key roles in the brewing process:

■ Alpha acids impart a bitter flavour and possess anti-bacterial properties. The level of alpha acids in a hop variety is measured as a percentage – the higher the figure, the higher the levels of bitterness that can be potentially extracted. Alpha acids are not soluble in water and therefore require boiling. The longer the boil time, the more alpha acids will be dissolved and the greater the final bitterness.

■ Beta acids impart aroma to a beer and do not require boiling. They contain highly volatile essential oils, which are driven off by the steam of the boil, so it is best to add them in the final minutes of the boil or once the boil is complete. These delicate acids can also be added during fermentation, a process known as dry hopping.

KEEPING HOPS FRESH

Dried hops react with light and air and so deteriorate relatively quickly. For this reason, they are usually supplied in light-protective, vacuum-sealed packets. You can store hops in un-opened packets for about two years, but once opened and exposed to the air they will quickly dry out and loose their delicate essential oils. As they are usually packed in 100g (3½oz) quantities, and many beers require several different varieties, you may end up with lots of half-used packs. To keep them fresh, simply seal and store in the freezer, using direct from frozen when required.

Add dried hops at various stages of the boil, depending on whether they are intended for bitterness, flavour, or aroma.

HOPS FOR BREWING

Fresh hops must be air-dried before they can be used in brewing. This helps preserve them and locks in the flavours and aromas. The recipes in this book call for dried whole-leaf hops, which have the most natural flavour, although they can deteriorate quickly if exposed to air. Processed hop pellets are a popular alternative and have a longer shelf life.

Dried whole-leaf hops

Hop pellets

HOPS – AT A GLANCE

Hop name	Country of origin	Alpha acid range	Character description	Flavour intensity (1 = low; 10 = high)
Admiral	UK	14–16%	Resinous, citrus, orange	9
Ahtanum	US	5–8%	Floral, citrus, lemon	7
Amarillo	US	7–11%	Floral, citrus, orange	9
Apollo	US	15–19%	Resinous, strong herbal	8
Atlas	Slovenia	5–9%	Lime, floral, pine	6
Aurora	Slovenia	5–9%	Lime, floral, pine	6
Bobek (Styrian Golding)	Slovenia	2–5%	Pine, lemon, floral	8
Bramling Cross	UK	5–8%	Spicy, blackcurrant	8
Brewer's Gold	Germany	5–9%	Spicy, blackcurrant, lemon	8
Cascade	US/UK/NZ	5–9%	Lychee, floral, grapefruit	9
Celia (Styrian Golding)	Slovenia	2–5%	Lemon, pine, floral	8
Centennial	US	7–12%	Lemon, herbal, resinous	9
Challenger	UK	5–9%	Spicy, cedar, green tea	7
Chinook	US	11–15%	Grapefruit, citrus, pine	9
Citra	US	11–14%	Mango, tropical fruit, lime	9
Cluster	US	6–9%	Blackberry, spicy	6
Columbus	US	14–20%	Sherbert, black pepper, liquorice	9
Crystal	US	3–6%	Tangerine, citrus	6
Delta	US	4–7%	Pineapple, pear	5
East Kent Golding	UK	5–8%	Spicy, honey, earthy	6
First Gold	UK	6–9%	Orange, marmalade, spicy	6
Fuggle	UK	4–7%	Grassy, minty, earthy	6
Galaxy	Australia	13–15%	Passionfruit, peaches	8
Galena	US	10–14%	Blackcurrant, spicy, grapefruit	6
Golding	UK	4–8%	Spicy, honey, earthy	6
Green Bullet	NZ	10–13%	Pine, raisin, black pepper	7
Hersbrucker	Germany	2–4%	Floral, herbal	6
Liberty	USA	3–5%	Spicy, lemon, citrus	6
Mittlefrüh	Germany	3–6%	Herbal, floral, grassy	6
Motueka	NZ	5–8%	Lemon, lime, floral	8
Mount Hood	US	4–7%	Herbal, grapefruit	6

Hop name	Country of origin	Alpha acid range	Character description	Intensity (1 = low; 10 = high)
Nelson Sauvin	NZ	10–13%	Gooseberry, grapefruit	9
Newport	US	13–17%	Cedar, fruity, herbal	7
Northdown	UK	6–9%	Spicy, cedar, pine	7
Northern Brewer	Germany	5–9%	Spicy, resinous, herbal	6
Nugget	US	10–14%	Spicy, pear, peach	6
Pacific Gem	NZ	13–18%	Blackberry, oak, pine	7
Pacific Jade	NZ	12–14%	Herbal, lemon zest, black pepper	8
Pacifica	NZ	4–8%	Herbal, orange, citrus	6
Palisade	US	6–10%	Citrus, blackcurrant, grapefruit	7
Perle	Germany	6–9%	Spicy, cedar, orange	7
Pilgrim	UK	9–12%	Spicy, cedar, honey	6
Pioneer	UK	9–12%	Cedar, grapefruit, herbal	8
Pride of Ringwood	Australia	9–12%	Cedar, oak, herbal	5
Progress	UK	5–8%	Spicy, honey, grassy	6
Riwaka	NZ	5–8%	Grapefruit, lime, tropical fruit	8
Saaz	Czech Republic	2–5%	Earthy, herbal, floral	5
Santiam	US	4–7%	Herbal, peach, lemon	6
Savinski (Styrian Golding)	Slovenia	2–4%	Lemon, lime, earthy	8
Simcoe	US	11–15%	Pine, grapefruit, passionfruit	6
Sorachi Ace	US	10–14%	Lemon, coconut	7
Sovereign	UK	4–7%	Grassy, floral, earthy	6
Spalt Select	Germany	2–5%	Herbal, floral, earthy	5
Summer	Australia	4–7%	Apricot, melon	6
Summit	US	13–15%	Pink grapefruit, orange	9
Target	UK	9–12%	Pine, cedar, liquorice	9
Tettnang	Germany	4–7%	Earthy, herbal, floral	5
Wai-ti	NZ	2–4%	Mandarin, lemon, lime zest	6
Wakatu	NZ	7–10%	Vanilla, floral, lime	7
Warrior	US	13–15%	Resinous, herbal, pine	6
WGV	UK	5–8%	Spicy, herbal, earthy	7
Willamette	US	4–7%	Blackcurrant, spicy, floral	6

Yeast

Yeast is the ingredient that turns the sweet wort produced from malt, hops, and water into beer. It is a single-celled life form and type of fungus.

Yeast has been used to create beer for thousands of years, but it wasn't until the development of the microscope in the 17th century that its existence was first noted. Prior to this, brewers had simply left their wort uncovered, with fermentation taking place thanks to wild yeast spores in the atmosphere. Then, in 1857, the French chemist and microbiologist Louis Pasteur proved the importance of yeast in fermentation. Pasteur's discovery changed the way beer was produced as it allowed brewers to gain greater control over the fermentation process.

YEAST AND BREWING

There are thought to be more than 1,500 different species of yeast in existence, but only one is used for brewing – *Saccharomyces cerevisiae*. When added to

Many Belgian beers are brewed with yeasts that impart complex fruit flavours as a by-product of fermentation.

wort, the yeast cells feed on the sugars and carbohydrates contained in the sweet liquid, and produce carbon dioxide and ethanol (alcohol) as a result. The yeast also produces several by-products that affect the flavour and aroma of the finished beer. The most common by-products are esters, fusel alcohols, and diacetyl:

■ Esters are chemical compounds that contribute important flavour characteristics – typically complex fruit characters. They are found in varying amounts in many types of beer, especially ales and Belgian-style beers. The amount of esters produced depends in part on the fermentation temperature – the higher the temperature, the more esters produced.

■ Fusel alcohols are a mixture of various alcohol compounds, and they create hot, spicy, notes in the finished beer. Although they can be found in many beer styles, if they become too noticeable they are generally considered to be a flaw. In fact, the word fusel is German for "bad liquor".

■ Like fusel alcohols, the presence of too much diacetyl is seen as a flaw in most beer styles, particularly lagers. Although it may exist in small, discreet amounts in many beers, in larger quantities it can deliver overpowering butter and butterscotch flavours and aromas. Diacetyl is usually "cleaned up" by the yeast once fermentation is complete, so its presence in the finished beer is often a sign of poor fermentation.

TOP- AND BOTTOM-FERMENTING YEASTS

There are two main types of yeast used in brewing: top-fermenting (for producing ales) and bottom-fermenting (for producing lagers).

Top-fermenting yeasts work best at higher fermentation temperatures, typically 16–24°C (60–75°F) and are so-called because they rise to the top of the fermenter during fermentation. These yeasts produce lots of complex esters, especially at higher temperatures, which results in a wide range of flavours and aromas. Top-fermenting yeasts are sub-divided into ale and wheat strains due to their distinct flavour characteristics.

Bottom-fermenting yeasts, on the other hand, work best at lower fermentation temperatures, typically 7–15°C (45–60°F), and settle out at the bottom of the fermenter. These yeasts tend to result in beers with a clean, neutral flavour. Due to the lower fermentation temperatures, they produce fewer esters but more diacetyl than top-fermenting yeasts. Many bottom-fermenting yeasts require a "diacetyl rest" (during which the temperature is raised for a few days at the end of fermentation), which helps reduce the levels of diacetyl.

FLOCCULATION AND ATTENUATION

All yeasts can be measured in terms of their flocculation and attenuation rates. Flocculation is a measure of how easily the yeast falls out of suspension in the wort, which affects how quickly and easily the beer will clear – the higher the flocculation rate, the quicker the beer will clear. Highly flocculating yeasts may need to be roused, or stirred, during fermentation to lift the particles back into suspension and so allow fermentation to complete successfully.

Attenuation is a measure of how efficiently the yeast will ferment the available sugars. It is usually measured as a percentage, with, for example, a 100-per-cent attenuation rate indicating that a yeast will ferment all the sugars in the wort to alcohol. Yeasts that have high attenuation rates generally have low flocculation rates, and vice versa.

REUSING YEAST

Although some yeasts – typically those in liquid form (see below) – are expensive, you can reuse them. Simply collect about 500ml (17½fl oz) of sediment from the bottom of the fermenter after fermentation is complete and store it in a sterilized container in the fridge. If used within a couple of weeks, you can pitch this yeast directly into your next batch of wort.

Don't worry if you leave it longer than two weeks, though, as you can still reuse yeast by making a starter (see pp62–63). Alternatively, time your brew days so that the sediment from one batch can be pitched into the wort of a new batch.

Liquid yeasts can be reused three or four times; dried yeasts are not suitable for reuse, but they are relatively inexpensive.

BREWER'S TIP

A great way of sourcing fresh liquid yeast is to visit your local microbrewery. They should have lots of left-over yeast on hand and should be happy to help.

If using liquid yeast, you will first need to make a yeast starter to increase the number of active cells.

FORMS OF YEAST

Yeasts for home brewing are available dried and in fresh liquid form. Dried yeast has a long shelf life and is easy to use, but the range can be limited. The main brands are Fermentis and Danstar. In contrast, there is a huge range of liquid yeasts available, allowing you to brew any beer you choose. Liquid yeast does, however, have a short shelf life and you will need to make a starter (see pp62–63). Wyeast and Whitelabs are the main brands.

Dried yeast

Fresh liquid yeast

Yeasts – at a glance

The availability of fresh yeast can vary, so use this chart to find alternative yeasts for some of the key recipes in the book (note that not all recipes can be accurately produced using dried yeast).

BEER STYLE	BEER NAME	LIQUID YEAST		DRIED YEAST
		Wyeast	Whitelabs	
Light Lager	European Lager (see p83)	2007 Pilsen Lager	830 German Lager	Fermentis 34/70
Light Lager	Premium American Lager (see p84)	2035 American Lager	800 Pilsner	Fermentis 34/70
Light Lager	Dortmunder Export (see pp86–87)	2124 Bohemian Lager	830 German Lager	Fermentis S23
Light Lager	Japanese Rice Lager (see p89)	2278 Czech Pils	800 Pilsner	Fermentis 34/70
Pilsner	Czech Pilsner (see pp90–91)	2001 Urquell	800 Pilsner	Fermentis 34/70
Pilsner	German Pilsner (see p93)	2007 Pilsen Lager	840 American Lager	Fermentis 34/70
Pilsner	American Pilsner (see p95)	2035 American Lager	840 American Lager	Fermentis 34/70
Amber Lager	Vienna Lager (see pp96–97)	2124 Bohemian Lager	830 German Lager	Fermentis 34/70
Amber Lager	Oktoberfest (see p98)	2206 Bavarian Lager	820 Oktoberfest	Fermentis 34/70
Bock	Helles Bock (see p99)	2487 Hella Bock	833 German Bock	Fermentis 34/70
Bock	Doppelbock (see p102)	2124 Bohemian Lager	830 German Lager	Fermentis 34/70
Bock	Eisbock (see p103)	2308 Munich Lager	838 Southern German Lager	Fermentis 34/70
Dark Lager	Munich Dunkel (see p106)	2278 Czech Pils	800 Pilsner	Fermentis 34/70
Dark Lager	Black Lager (see p107)	2042 Danish Lager	860 Munich Helles	Fermentis S23
Pale Ale	Spring Beer (see p112)	1275 Thames Valley Ale	023 Burton Ale	Danstar Nottingham
Pale Ale	Harvest Ale (see p114)	1272 American Ale II	060 American Ale Blend	Fermentis US05
Pale Ale	ESB (see p115)	1187 Ringwood Ale	005 English Ale	Fermentis S04
Pale Ale	Pale Ale (see pp122–23)	1187 Ringwood Ale	005 English Ale	Danstar Nottingham
Pale Ale	Honey Ale (see p124)	1098 British Ale	007 Dry English Ale	Danstar Nottingham

BEER STYLE	BEER NAME	LIQUID YEAST		DRIED YEAST
		Wyeast	**Whitelabs**	
IPA	English IPA (see p131)	1187 Ringwood	005 English Ale	Fermentis US05
IPA	American IPA (see p133)	1272 American Ale II	060 American Ale Blend	Fermentis US05
IPA	Black IPA (see p136)	1187 Ringwood Ale	005 English Ale	Fermentis US05
Bitter	London Bitter (see p140)	1318 London Ale III	013 London Ale	Fermentis S04
Bitter	Irish Red Ale (see p149)	1084 Irish Ale	004 Irish Ale	Fermentis S33
Strong Ale	Winter Warmer (see p150)	1968 ESB	002 English Ale	Fermentis S04
Strong Ale	Bière de Garde (see pp152–53)	3711 French Saison	566 Saison II	N/A
Strong Ale	Belgian Blonde (see p155)	1388 Belgian Strong	570 Belgian Golden Ale	N/A
Strong Ale	Belgian Dubbel (see p156)	3944 Belgian Witbier	400 Belgian Wit Ale	Fermentis WB06
Brown Ale	Southern Brown Ale (see p161)	1187 Ringwood Ale	005 English Ale	Fermentis US05
Mild	Mild (see p164)	1318 London Ale III	013 London	Fermentis US05
Barley Wine	English Barley Wine (see pp166–67)	1028 London	013 London	Fermentis S33
Barley Wine	American Barley Wine (see p168)	1056 American Ale	001 California Ale	Fermentis S33
Stout	Dry Stout (see p174)	1084 Irish Ale	004 Irish Ale	Fermentis US05
Porter	Brown Porter (see p169)	1028 London Ale	013 London Ale	Fermentis US05
Wiessbier	Wiezenbock (see p185)	3056 Bavarian Wheat	380 Hefeweizen IV	Danstar Munich
Rye Beer	Roggenbier (see p188)	3338 Bavarian Wheat	380 Hefeweizen IV	fermentis WB06
Witbier	Witbier (see pp190–91)	3944 Belgian Witbier	400 Belgian Wit Ale	fermentis WB06
Dark Wheat Beer	Dunkelweizen (see p192)	3056 Bavarian Wheat	380 Hefeweizen IV	fermentis WB06
Light hybrid	Kölsch (see p197)	2565 Kölsch	029 German Ale	Fermentis US05
Amber hybrid	Californian Common (see p198)	2112 California Ale	810 San Francisco Lager	Fermentis US05

Brewing liquor

Water – known as liquor by brewers – is the main ingredient in beer. As a result, the quality and chemical profile of the water you use can have a noticeable effect on the finished beer.

The chemical make up of your water supply depends on the journey it takes to reach your tap. As rainwater (all of our water starts off as rainwater) precipitates through the ground, it can pick up various minerals, depending on the type of rock it passes through. Some minerals, such as calcium and magnesium, are soluble in water. Known as ions, these soluble minerals are absorbed into the water supply. Water with a high mineral content is classified as hard, while water with a low mineral content – typically water that passes through rock such as slate or granite – is classified as soft.

BEER STYLES AND WATER
Before chemical analysis of water was available, beer styles were often dictated by the chemical make up of the local water supply. If you want to reproduce a certain style of beer, replicating the water from that region will help you achieve authentic results. For example, the water profile of the Pilsen region of the Czech Republic – the home of Pilsner lagers – has some of the softest water in the world, with almost no mineral content. This results in exceptionally clear, clean-tasting lagers. By contrast, Dublin in Ireland – the home of Guinness, the famous dry stout – has very hard water containing high levels of bicarbonates and calcium. This gives the water a high pH, which is then balanced out by the acidity of the highly roasted malts to create the perfect stout.

KIT AND MALT-EXTRACT BREWING
For kit and malt-extract brewing (see pp54–57), the chemical make up of your water will have only a minor effect on the finished beer – if the water tastes and smells good, it should produce good beer. The only potential cause for concern is if your water supplier

Soft water produces light lagers with a crisp, clean taste

The best stouts are brewed using hard water, which has a high pH adds high levels of chlorine or chloramine, as these antibacterial chemicals can react with the yeast and create unwanted medicinal flavours (see below for simple water treatments).

FULL-MASH BREWING

For full-mash brewing (see pp58–61), the chemical make up of your water becomes much more important. Specifically, during the mash (see p59) the pH level of your water supply (it's acidity or alkalinity) will effect the efficiency of the enzymes in the malt (see pp22–23). Most malts work best at a pH level of 5.2 (where 1 is the most acidic and 14 the most alkaline).

Later, during fermentation, the pH levels will naturally drop as the yeast ferments the sugars in the wort. This has the benefit of creating a more unfriendly environment for unwanted bacteria. Getting the pH levels right can also help with the clarity and overall quality of the finished beer.

WATER ANALYSIS

In brewing terms, the important ions in water are calcium, magnesium, bicarbonate, sodium, chloride and sulfate. Your water company should be able to provide a report that gives a chemical breakdown of the local water supply. You can then add calcium sulphate (gypsum), magnesium sulphate, or sodium to alter these levels as necessary – to adjust the pH levels required for a specific recipe. Working out these additions and adjustments can be complicated, but there are several calculators online that will make the various calculations for you (see p213 for more information).

Digital pH tester

TESTING THE MASH

Simply use a pH strip or digital pH reader to measure the mash pH, then record the results so you can adjust the water for the next brew. It is worth remembering, however, that while it is useful to know the profile of your water profile in full-mash brewing when emulating a certain beer style, you can still make great beer with only basic preparation.

If your water supply has high levels of chlorine, boil it for about 30 minutes before use

SIMPLE WATER TREATMENTS

If, for example, your water is hard and you want to brew a full-mash lager or Pilsner recipe that requires soft water, you could simply mix your tap water with a large proportion of distilled or de-ionised water, which is available to buy. This will help maintain the correct mash pH and avoid astringent tannin flavours being introduced to the finished beer.

To remove chlorine, you can either leave the water you will need for brewing to stand overnight, or you can boil it for 30 minutes before use. Chloramine, however, cannot be removed by boiling. The easiest way to remove both chlorine and chloramine is to add a crushed Campden tablet to your water a few minutes before using.

For kit and malt-extract brewers, the most important consideration is that your water is free from chlorine and chloramine – and if you are lucky enough to have great-tasting water straight from the tap, there is no need to treat it at all.

BREWER'S TIP

An alternative to treating your own tap water is to use bottled mineral water. Although this is more expensive, bottled water is convenient and ideal for brewing.

Herbs, flowers, fruits, and spices

Originally used in place of hops to add flavour and protect the beer from bacteria, you can use any of these ingredients to introduce a range of fascinating flavours and aromas.

CARDAMOM SEEDS
Popular in Belgian-style beers, cardamom complements coriander, cumin, and citrus flavours. Add in the last few minutes of the boil or about four days into fermentation.

CORIANDER SEEDS
This works well alongside bitter orange in Witbiers, imparting a distinctive flavour. Add in the last few minutes of the boil or about four days into fermentation.

STAR ANISE
Use star anise in Belgian-style ales and festive brews to add a pungent, sweet flavour. Add in the last few minutes of the boil or about four days into fermentation.

CINNAMON STICKS
Cinnamon imparts a distinctively festive aroma and flavour, so use it in dark, full-bodied beers. Add in the last few minutes of the boil or about four days into fermentation.

LIQUORICE ROOT
This imparts a distinctive, sweet flavour for use in strong festive and vintage beers. Add in the last few minutes of the boil or about four days into fermentation.

VANILLA PODS
Use just one or two vanilla pods in stout and porter recipes to add a sweet, warm flavour. Add in the last few minutes of the boil or about four days into fermentation.

CHILLI PEPPERS
Use in Mexican beers and light lagers to add a subtle, dry aftertaste and a slight burn; also great for novelty beers. Add about four days into fermentation.

JUNIPER BERRIES
The main flavouring in gin, you can also add juniper to beers for a subtle gin-like flavour. Add in the last few minutes of the boil or about four days into fermentation.

ROSE HIPS
Use rose hips sparingly to lend character to festive and strong beers. Add in the last few minutes of the boil or about four days into fermentation.

ELDERBERRIES
Popular in wine making, elderberries introduce a port-like flavour that works well in strong festive beers. Add a small amount about four days into fermentation.

ELDERFLOWERS
Great in summer ales, elderflowers can be overpowering so use in small amounts. Add in the last few minutes of the boil or about four days into fermentation.

KAFFIR LIME LEAVES
With a spicy flavour and aroma, kaffir lime leaves will also introduce a clean, citrus flavour. Add in the last few minutes of the boil or about four days into fermentation.

STRAWBERRIES
Use a few strawberries in pale beers and lagers for a subtle sweetness. Add about four days into fermentation.

RASPBERRIES
These work well in Belgian wheat and sour beers to impart a sweet, fruity character. Add approximately four days into fermentation.

CHERRIES
Popular in Belgian-style Kriek beers, cherries balance the alcohol and bitterness. Add about four days into fermentation.

ORANGE PEEL
Use sweet orange peel in strong Belgian and festive beers for a Cointreau-style character. Bitter orange peel (or Curuçao) adds zesty orange flavours to Belgian and wheat beers but, despite the name, no bitterness. Add in the last few minutes of the boil or about four days into fermentation.

Lemon peel

Lime peel

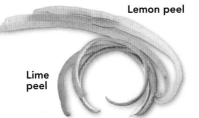

LEMON AND LIME PEEL
Lemon peel works well in pale ales and light summer beers, adding a zesty, citrus character. Lime peel also works well in pale ales, where it complements coriander and lemongrass and gives a refreshing zing. Add in the last few minutes of the boil or about four days into fermentation.

HEATHER TIPS
Traditionally used in Scottish ales known as Fraoch, heather imparts a grassy, minty aroma and flavour. Traditionally, heather tips were often added in beer recipes instead of hops due to their bittering qualities. Add in the last few minutes of the boil or about four days into fermentation.

Getting started

Before you begin

Brewing your own beer should be an enjoyable and rewarding experience. To make sure the process runs smoothly, there are four key factors to consider before you start.

WHAT STYLE OF BEER DO YOU WANT TO BREW?

You should be able to recreate at home any style of beer available commercially. However, due to the processes involved, some styles require additional equipment and more advanced techniques. If you are new to brewing, start with a relatively simple recipe such as a pale ale (see pp112–30), bitter (see pp140–49), or stout (see pp174–81). Lager recipes (see pp82–107) are usually more complicated to produce as they need to be fermented and stored at cooler temperatures. If you do decide to brew a lager, acquiring an old fridge and connecting it to a digital temperature controller (see p53) will allow you to regulate the temperature for the best results.

(see pp112–30), (see pp140–49), (see pp174–81), (see pp82–107), (see p53)

TIPS FOR SUCCESSFUL HOME BREWING

- Check that you have the required equipment and ingredients before you start.
- Create a checklist so you know what to do at every stage.
- When buying ingredients, order extra packets of dried yeast, malt extract, and brewing sugar – this could prevent a whole batch of beer going to waste should the yeast fail, for example, or if extra sugar is required.
- Brew days can take longer than anticipated, especially when using the full-mash method, so start early.
- Consider teaming up with a friend – it's more fun, and you can split the costs and share the workload.
- Don't start sampling previous batches of beer until you've finished brewing for the day!

Start off with an ale recipe, as they are quick and easy brews

Lagers require more skill and equipment than most ale recipes

WHICH METHOD ARE YOU GOING TO USE?

There are three main ways to produce beer at home – using a kit, malt extract, or the full-mash method (see pp44–45). The method you choose will determine the type of equipment and ingredients you will need to buy before you start.

The simplest way to make beer is from a kit. These are great for beginners as they are simple to use and produce high-quality beer. Don't worry if you move on to more advanced methods – the equipment needed for making beer with a kit is also required for malt-extract and full-mash brewing, so your investment won't be wasted.

The malt-extract method is also straightforward and will allow you to brew a wider range of beers. Many of the recipes in this book feature malt-extract variations.

Kits are quick, easy, and can produce professional-tasting beer

WHERE ARE YOU GOING TO BREW?

Brewing can be a messy job so choosing the right room in the house in which to make your beer is an important decision. For most people, the kitchen is the best place to prepare the wort, as there is easy access to fresh water, drainage, and a heat source. Alternatively, as lots of strong-smelling steam will be created when boiling malt-extract and full-mash recipes, an outside space may be preferable.

Once you have created a wort, you will need to find a suitable place to leave 27 litres (47½ pints) of liquid to ferment at a constant temperature and away from direct sunlight. Most ale yeasts, for example, require a warm ambient temperature, so you may need a heater (see p50) if brewing in a cold place.

You may decide to simply boil the wort on an ordinary kitchen hob

FIND A GOOD SUPPLIER

As you experiment with brewing your own beer, you will need equipment, ingredients, and perhaps some friendly advice – so finding a good supplier is key. If you are lucky enough to have a specialist supplier locally, pay them a visit. Most will be more than happy to offer advice. Look for a supplier with a good range of yeasts (including liquid varieties), vacuum-packed hops, and equipment.

If you don't have a home-brew store in your area, there are several online retailers who will be able to supply equipment and ingredients. They should be able to provide advice and support if needed. Online forums are also a great way to pick up tips and share your experiences with other home brewers.

With a wide range of ingredients you can experiment with different beer styles

Three methods of brewing

Brewing beer at home can be as easy or involved as you wish. There are three main ways of making up a wort – each method more advanced than the last.

METHOD 1 – USING A KIT

Brewing using a kit (see pp54–55 for step-by-step techniques) is the simplest way to make beer at home. A wort is prepared in advance by a malt producer, who then removes most of the water to create a small volume of concentrated, treacle-like liquid. This is re-hydrated by the home brewer to make up the volume for a full batch of beer. It takes only 20–30 minutes and requires no prior knowledge. The quality of home-brew kits has improved greatly in recent years, with professional breweries developing kits that closely replicate their commercial beers.

ADVANTAGES	DISADVANTAGES
■ Quick to prepare ■ Simple to use and requires no prior knowledge ■ Requires only basic equipment	■ Offers little scope to customize a recipe ■ Any hop aroma is likely to have been lost during the production process

METHOD 2 – USING MALT EXTRACT

Brewing with malt extract (see pp56–57 for step-by-step techniques) involves adding unhopped malt extract – either in liquid or dried form – to water and boiling it with hops, which are added at various intervals. The wort is then cooled to produce a fermentable wort. This method is more involved than using a kit and requires additional equipment (see pp48–53), but you will be rewarded for the effort as malt-extract brewing is highly regarded in brewing circles and can produce award-winning beers.

ADVANTAGES	DISADVANTAGES
■ A variety of beers and styles can be produced ■ Speciality grains can be used for flavour ■ You are more involved in the process so will gain confidence and knowledge	■ Not all malts are available in extract form ■ It is the most expensive method, due to the high cost of malt extract ■ Requires additional time and equipment

METHOD 3 – FULL-MASH BREWING

The full-mash method, also known as all-grain brewing, is the technique used in professional breweries. It consists of three key processes – the mash, sparge, and boil (see pp58–61 for step-by-step techniques). Full-mash brewing offers maximum flexibility and allows you to replicate any style of beer. It does, however, require the most knowledge, equipment, time, and effort, and so is not suitable for everyone. Typically, a home brewer advances through the first two methods, gaining experience and confidence, before moving on to full-mash brewing.

ADVANTAGES	DISADVANTAGES
■ No limit to the number of styles that can be produced ■ Uses the cheapest ingredients ■ Offers complete control over ingredients used ■ Produces the highest quality beer	■ Requires the most amount of equipment ■ Brewing can take several hours ■ Can generate a lot of mess ■ More things can go wrong!

Three-tiered full-mash brewing set-up

Full-mash brewers typically use three separate vessels – a hot liquor tank or HLT for heating and storing all the water (known as liquor by brewers), a mash tun for mixing malted grain with hot water to produce a sweet wort, and a boiler for boiling the wort with hops to sterilize it and add flavour and aroma. In a home environment, the flow of water and wort is usually achieved via gravity using a tiered set-up. Side-by-side systems can also be used, but a pump would be required.

Hot liquor tank
(HLT)

Mash tun

Boiler

Brew-in-a-bag full-mash method

Full-mash brews can also be produced in a single boiling vessel, known as the brew in a bag or BIAB method. All the water is heated to mash temperature in a boiler, grains are added in a bag for the mash, and then the bag is removed before the boil. The set-up costs are cheaper and the process is quicker and less messy than a typical full-mash brew, but you will need a very large boiling vessel and the mashing process is not as efficient at extracting fermentable sugars from the grains.

The importance of sanitation

The key to producing great beer is to pay proper attention to sanitation. In fact, commercial brewers spend as much time cleaning and sterilizing equipment as they do brewing beer.

Poor sanitation is the biggest cause of spoiled batches of beer. While prepared wort is the ideal environment for propagating yeast cells, it is also the perfect host for unfriendly, wild bacteria – and once a beer has become contaminated it usually can not be saved. Good sanitation is particularly important during the warmer summer months, when there is a greater risk from airborne bacteria.

CLEANING AND STERILIZING

Good sanitation means thoroughly cleaning and sterilizing all your brewing equipment. Get into the habit of cleaning equipment immediately after use – dirt and debris is much easier to remove before it has had a chance to dry. Also, remember to remove the taps from your vessels and carefully scrub the threads, as this is a common problem area.

Once cleaned, equipment must be sterilized to kill off any bacteria. Every piece of equipment that comes into contact with the wort after the boil must be sterilized, including trial jars, hydrometers, thermometers, and spoons. Depending on the type of sterilizer you decide to use (see opposite), you may have to rinse it off afterwards.

For convenience, sterilize small pieces of equipment inside the fermenter

CLEANING BOTTLES

This can be an arduous task, especially if yeast sediment has dried at the bottom (washing out your bottles as soon as the beer inside them has been drunk will save you a lot of time and effort later on). If the bottles are very soiled, soak them in a light bleach solution for an hour. Then remove the dirt and debris using a bottle brush, and sanitize and rinse the bottles.

Bottle brushes

ACID-BASED STERILIZERS

Suitable for use on most materials, including stainless steel, acid-based sterilizers are easy to use, work very quickly – often in as little as 30 seconds – and require minimum rinsing. In fact, the most popular brand, a foaming product called Star San, doesn't need to be rinsed off at all. Star San does, however, require a water pH of less than 3.5 (see pp36–37 for more about water), so you may need to use distilled water. You will know if the pH of your water is too high as it will turn cloudy when the sterilizer is added.

CHLORINE-BASED STERILIZERS

Products containing chorine are so effective at killing bacteria that only a tiny amount is needed. A solution of just 1 millilitre of pure chlorine diluted in 1,000 litres of water (or 0.02fl oz diluted in 1,000 pints) would be adequate. Note that chlorine-based products are not suitable for soaking stainless-steel vessels as they will cause pitting over time. You should also rinse with hot water after use.

Specialist chlorine-based products, in both liquid and powder form, are available. These are typically very easy to use – just follow individual product usage guidelines.

Household bleach

The most common source of chlorine is household bleach, which is about 5 per cent pure chlorine. Prepare a solution of 0.5ml of bleach per litre of water (0.01fl oz of bleach per pint of water) and leave the vessels and equipment to soak for up to 30 minutes. For stubborn residues, use a stronger solution of up to 3ml per litre (or 0.07fl oz per pint) and leave to soak overnight. Avoid scented bleaches as they can impart unwanted aromas.

IODINE-BASED STERILIZERS

Idophor is the most common iodine-based product and can be a very effective sterilizer. Like chlorine, iodine products will cause pitting on stainless steel if left in contact for extended periods of time. They also have a faint brown colour, which can cause staining to plastic products – although this looks unattractive, it is not a problem.

A NOTE ON SODIUM METABISULFITE

Although some home brewers use sodium metabisulfite (also known as Campden tablets) to sterilize their brewing equipment, the practice is not recommended. Bacteria growth will not be sufficiently inhibited by the chemical and your beer may still become contaminated.

Sodium metabisulfite is better suited for wine and cider making, in which levels of acidity are higher and the chemical causes sulphur dioxide to be produced (sulphur dioxide is effective at killing off wild bacteria). Wines and ciders typically have higher levels of alcohol, too, which further helps prevent contamination.

BREWER'S TIP

Scratches in your equipment provide ideal hiding places for bacteria, so make regular checks and replace equipment as necessary.

Chlorine-based sterilizer (liquid)

Chlorine-based sterilizer (powder)

Acid-based sterilizer

Brewing equipment

The basic equipment you need to make beer at home is affordable and can be used for all three methods of brewing – although malt-extract and full-mash brewing do require more equipment than kit brewing.

BREWING EQUIPMENT – AT A GLANCE

Equipment	Kit brewing	Malt-extract brewing	Full-mash brewing
Fermenter (see opposite)	✓	✓	✓
Hydrometer and trial jar (see opposite)	✓	✓	✓
Siphon (see opposite)	✓	✓	✓
Brewer's spoon (see opposite)	✓	✓	✓
Thermometer (see p50)	✓	✓	✓
Storage container (see p50 and pp68–69)	✓	✓	✓
Can opener and kettle (see p50)	✓	N/A	N/A
Airlock (see p50)	OPTIONAL	OPTIONAL	OPTIONAL
Heater (see p50)	OPTIONAL	OPTIONAL	OPTIONAL
Bottle-filling stick (see p50)	OPTIONAL	OPTIONAL	OPTIONAL
Boiler (see p51)	N/A	✓	✓
Weighing scales (see p51)	N/A	✓	✓
Digital timer (see p51)	N/A	✓	✓
Grain bags (see p51)	N/A	OPTIONAL	OPTIONAL
Chiller (see p51)	N/A	OPTIONAL	OPTIONAL
Mash tun (see p52)	N/A	N/A	✓
Sparge arm (see p52)	N/A	N/A	✓
Hot liquor tank (see p52)	N/A	N/A	✓
Hop back (see p53)	N/A	OPTIONAL	OPTIONAL
Erlenmeyer flask (see p53)	N/A	OPTIONAL	OPTIONAL
Stir plate (see p53)	N/A	OPTIONAL	OPTIONAL
Beer gun (see p53)	N/A	OPTIONAL	OPTIONAL
Digital temperature controller and brew fridge (see p53)	N/A	OPTIONAL	OPTIONAL
Brewing software and applications (see p53)	N/A	N/A	OPTIONAL
Digital pH meter (see p53)	N/A	N/A	OPTIONAL
Refractometer (see p53)	N/A	N/A	OPTIONAL

FERMENTATION VESSELS

All home brewers need a suitable fermentation vessel in which to ferment their wort. There are three main types of fermenter:

■ **Plastic "bucket" fermenter**
This is the most popular type. It is inexpensive, durable, easy to clean, and available in several sizes – from 5 litres (8¾ pints) right up to 210 litres (370 pints). Some plastic fermenters are supplied with an airlock and tap.

■ **Glass carboy**
Also known as a demijohn, the benefits of this popular type of fermenter are that it won't scratch easily, become stained, or taint the beer with unwanted flavours. It also allows you to see the yeast as it ferments. However, glass carboys can be very heavy when full and are awkward to clean.

■ **Stainless-steel fermenter**
This is very hard wearing, easy to clean, and will protect the beer from sunlight. Many have a conical bottom, which allows the yeast to settle out of the wort. They are, however, the most expensive type.

BREWER'S SPOON

A long spoon is essential for stirring large vessels of wort when combining ingredients, and for introducing oxygen prior to pitching the yeast. Stainless steel spoons are easiest to keep clean and free from bacteria.

HYDROMETER AND TRIAL JAR

A hydrometer is an instrument used for measuring the specific gravity, or density, of a liquid. Comprising a glass stem with a scale, and with a weighted bulb at one end, it is placed in a sample of beer (collected in a trial jar) where it floats at a particular level depending on the gravity of the beer. As alcohol is less dense than sugar, a hydrometer will float at a

Glass carboy

Plastic fermenter   *Airlock*   *Tap* ⋯⋯

Stainless steel brewer's spoon

lower level as the fermentation process progresses. By taking a reading before fermentation (original gravity or OG) and one afterwards (final gravity or FG), you can both determine when fermentation has finished and calculate the alcohol content of the beer (see p63 for more about taking gravity readings and calculating alcohol content).

SIPHON

A siphon allows you to transfer beer by removing it from the top of a vessel, rather than draining it from the bottom – leaving any sediment undisturbed at the bottom. A siphon can be as simple as a length of plastic tubing. Some types have a sediment trap at one

end, which prevents residue being sucked up by mistake, and a tap at the other end to control the flow.

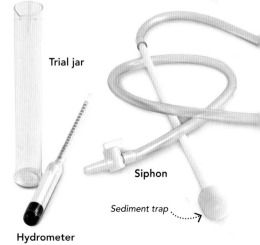

Trial jar

Siphon

Sediment trap ⋯⋯

Hydrometer

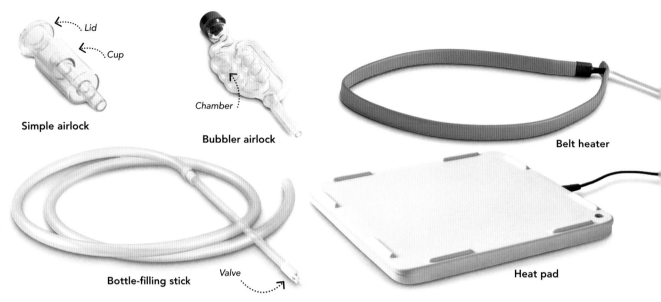

Simple airlock

Bubbler airlock

Chamber

Lid

Cup

Belt heater

Bottle-filling stick

Valve

Heat pad

AIRLOCKS

An airlock is a one-way valve that is fitted to the top of a sealed fermenter using a bung or rubber grommet. It allows carbon dioxide to escape as pressure builds up during fermentation, but prevents bacteria in the open air from reaching the wort. There are two main types:

■ **Bubbler airlock**

Also known as a chamber airlock, this consists of a series of water-filled chambers. The water acts as a barrier between the beer and the open air, but allows CO_2 to bubble through (meaning you can clearly see when fermentation has begun.

■ **Simple airlock**

Also known as a handy airlock, this type consists of a small plastic cup with a separate lid. The lid dislodges when the pressure in the fermenter builds up, allowing CO_2 to escape, but remains in place over the cup to prevent bacteria from entering. It is easier to clean than a bubbler airlock as the parts can be separated easily and cleaned with a small brush.

BOTTLE-FILLING STICK

Comprising a hollow plastic stick with a valve at the tip, this device releases beer on demand – preventing spillage when bottling.

HEATERS

If the ambient temperature where you intend to ferment your brew is too low, use one of these heaters:

■ **Belt heater**

This wraps around the fermenter. Although it is the cheapest type of heater, you will not be able to adjust the heat.

■ **Heat pad**

Sit this type of heater on the floor and place the fermenter on top. It heats to a set temperature above the ambient temperature.

■ **Immersion heater**

You will need to submerge this heater into the wort. The most expensive option, it has an adjustable thermostat for accurate temperature control.

THERMOMETERS

All home brewers need a thermometer to monitor the temperature of the wort during fermentation. Malt-extract and full-mash brewers will also need one when preparing hot water for steeping, mashing, and sparging. There are three main types:

■ **Glass spirit thermometer**

This is cheap, accurate, versatile, and the most popular type.

■ **Self-adhesive thermometer**

This liquid-crystal thermometer can be fixed to the outside of the fermenter for easy monitoring.

■ **Digital thermometer**

This is the easiest type of thermometer to use and read, but is also the most expensive.

STORAGE CONTAINER

All brewers will need a container (or containers) in which to store their beer while it matures. This could be a pressure barrel, keg, cask, or bottles (see pp68–69 for more about storage).

CAN OPENER AND KETTLE

Kit brewers will need a can opener (most kits are in canned form) and a kitchen kettle for adding boiling water to the fermenter when dissolving the malt extract.

Additional equipment for malt-extract and full-mash brewing

BOILERS

For malt-extract and full-mash brewing you will need a vessel in which to boil large volumes of liquid. Boilers may be made from plastic (cheap and easy to clean), stainless steel (hard wearing and easy to clean), or enamel (hard wearing and won't become stained). You should choose a boiler with enough "head space" at the top to avoid boil-overs – to boil a 23-litre (40-pint) batch you will need a boiler with a capacity of 30 litres (53 pints). Heat is provided by a built-in electric element or via a separate gas burner (most kitchen gas hobs are not powerful enough to maintain a vigorous boil).

CHILLER

A chiller enables you to cool large volumes of hot wort quickly and efficiently. A rapid cool reduces the risk of bacterial infection and creates a "cold break", in which proteins in the wort coagulate and sink to the bottom of the boiler where they are less likely to be transferred to the fermenter. There are two main types of chiller:

■ Immersion chiller

This comprises a coil of copper or stainless steel piping that you submerge in the hot wort. Tubing connected to each end of the coil allows cold water to be passed through for cooling. It can chill 23 litres (40 pints) of near-boiling wort to fermentation temperature (about 20°C/68°F) in approximately 30 minutes.

■ Counterflow chiller

This consists of a series of metal plates mounted inside a sealed unit. You pass cold water through a channel on one side of the unit and hot wort through a separate

Stainless-steel boiler

Built-in electric element ..... ↑ **Plastic boiler**

Copper piping ·······↘

Plastic tubing ·······↘

Immersion chiller

channel on the other side of the unit. The metal plates in between act as heat exchangers and cool the wort. Counterflow chillers may require an additional pump, are difficult to clean, and are more expensive than immersion chillers.

WEIGHING SCALES

You will need to weigh out each grain and hop addition for malt-extract and full-mash recipes. Digital scales are sensitive enough to give precise measurements for very small hop additions.

DIGITAL TIMER

This is used to remind you when to make each hop addition.

GRAIN BAGS

Grain bags are a convenient way of adding and removing speciality grains when steeping.

Additional equipment for full-mash brewing

MASH TUN

A mash tun is the vessel in which you combine and steep grains and hot water during the mash (see p59). A good mash tun should be well insulated and capable of maintaining a constant temperature for the duration of the mash – losing no more than 1°C (1.8°F) over a 90-minute period. Many mash tuns are simply plastic picnic-style cool boxes fitted with a tap and a grain strainer. These are widely available from home-brew suppliers. Alternatively, you could customize a cool box yourself. Stainless-steel tuns are harder wearing and easier to keep clean than plastic ones.

ROTATING SPARGE ARM

Used for rinsing the grains during the sparge (see p60), a rotating sparge arm works just like a sprinkler. Comprising a hollow stainless-steel tube with tiny holes along its length, it rotates freely when you flow sparge water through it, adding a fine spray across the surface of the grain. A support bar allows it to be placed across the top of the mash tun.

HOT LIQUOR TANK (HLT)

This vessel is used to heat and store the brewing liquor, or water, required for the various stages of full-mash brewing – the mash, sparge, and boil (see pp58–61). Although you can use a boiler (see p51) to heat and store water too, it is usually quicker and more convenient to use a separate vessel. A hot liquor tank is particularly useful, for example, if you are treating your liquor beforehand (see pp36–37), as it allows you to prepare and store the total volume in advance. For this reason, the HLT will need to be larger than the boiler, although the heating system doesn't have to be as powerful as it will only be used to heat water to mash and sparge temperature and not to a boil.

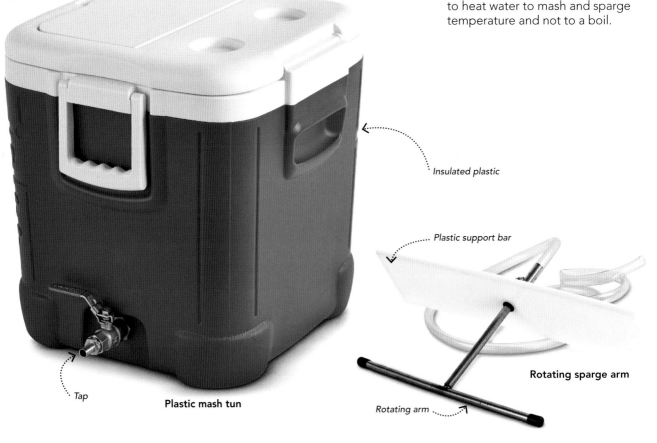

Insulated plastic

Plastic support bar

Rotating sparge arm

Tap

Plastic mash tun

Rotating arm

Advanced equipment

REFRACTOMETER

Accurate and simple to use, this is an optical instrument used to measure the density of a liquid based on its refractive index. You need only add a few drops of liquid to the device's optical prism, and you can use it instead of a hydrometer and trial jar (see p49) to determine the specific gravity of your beer. Most refractometers automatically adjust for temperature, making them ideal for taking gravity readings of hot wort while sparging (see p60).

DIGITAL PH TESTER

Advanced full-mash brewers will find it useful to be able to measure the acidity of the mash. Digital pH testers are simple to use and calibrate, give an accurate reading, and are easier to read than paper pH tester strips.

ERLENMEYER FLASK

An Erlenmeyer flask – named after the German chemist Emil Erlenmeyer – is a conical-shaped vessel useful for making yeast starters (see pp62–63). It allows you to combine, heat, and ferment the starter in a single vessel, and the conical shape means you can shake it to introduce oxygen without the contents spilling out. Choose a flask that is at least 1 litre (1¾ pints) larger than the starter volume.

HOP BACK

A hop back is a type of infuser used for extracting delicate hop oils and aromas that would

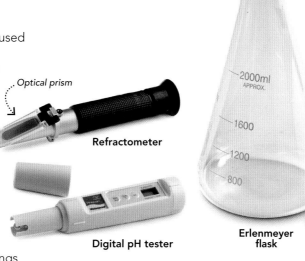

Optical prism

Refractometer

Digital pH tester

Erlenmeyer flask

Hop back

otherwise be lost during the boil. At the end of the boil, you divert the wort through the unit before running it into a counterflow chiller (see p51), where the wort is cooled and the aromas "locked-in". Used mainly by micro- and commercial brewers, hop backs are extremely effective at delivering a strong hoppy character from a small amount of hops. A version specially developed for home brewing – called the HopRocket – will allow you to achieve professional results.

DIGITAL TEMPERATURE CONTROLLER AND BREW FRIDGE

By controlling the fermentation temperature you can create a wide range of beer styles and achieve consistent results. Many home brewers store the fermenter in an old fridge that has been fitted with a heater – both are then connected to a temperature controller. The controller turns on the fridge as a cooler or heater as required.

BREWING SOFTWARE AND APPLICATIONS

When creating your own malt-extract or full-mash beer recipes, computer software and applications are ideal for making the necessary bitterness, colour, and gravity calculations. Many applications create worksheets that help you to plan your brew day, and some even produce shopping lists of ingredients (see p213 for details of online resources).

STIR PLATE

Comprising a metal bar, which is placed inside a fermentation vessel where it is moved by magnetic force, this is used to continuously agitate liquid-yeast starters (see pp62–63).

BEER GUN

This device allows you to transfer beer that has been stored and carbonated in a keg to bottles, without the need to add priming sugar (see p66) – thereby minimizing sediment.

Using a kit

Home-brew kits are a great introduction to the brewing process. They are quick, easy, and require only basic knowledge. With a little care, a kit will produce great-tasting beer in a matter of weeks.

Most kits make about 23 litres (40 pints) of beer, although stronger beers may be brewed in smaller volumes for greater concentration and a higher starting gravity. Before you begin, check that all the ingredients are present and within their use-by dates, and that you have the right equipment. Read the instructions and check how much water needs to be added.

THREE MAIN TYPES OF KIT

■ One-can liquid kits consist of a single can (or plastic pack) of hopped malt extract. These require extra sugar or malt extract to increase the amount of fermentable sugars to reach the correct starting gravity.

■ Two-can liquid kits (see step-by-step sequence) contain twice the amount of liquid malt and do not require additional sugar. They produce fuller-bodied, more professional-tasting beers than other types of kit.

■ Dried-malt kits contain powdered malt extract and may require additional sugar or malt extract. Always check the instructions first.

EQUIPMENT
- Large pan
- Can opener
- Fermenter
- Brewer's spoon or paddle
- Hydrometer and trial jar
- Thermometer
- Airlock (optional)

INGREDIENTS
- 1 or 2 cans liquid malt extract, or 1 packet dried malt (as supplied)
- 1 packet brewer's yeast
- Additional sugar, malt extract, hops, or fruit (if required)

PREPARATION ⏰ 20 MINS

1 Place the cans of malt extract in a pan of hot water. This will soften the liquid and make it easier to pour. While the cans are warming, thoroughly sterilize all your equipment (see pp44–45).

2 Open the cans and empty the contents into the fermenter. Add a kettleful of boiling water to the fermenter. Put on a pair of oven gloves and rinse out the cans with a little extra boiling water.

3 **Add cold water** to make up the required volume, pouring it in from a height to create a splash, then stir vigorously. This will oxygenate the wort and encourage the yeast to multiply quickly for healthy fermentation.

4 **Take a sample of the wort** with a sterilized trial jar (you could use a "beer thief" or turkey baster, if you have one, to extract the wort). Take a reading with a hydrometer (see p65) – this is the original gravity.

PITCHING THE YEAST ⏰ 5 MINS ⟫⟫

5 **Measure the temperature** of the wort in the fermenter. If it is warmer than 24°C (75°F), close the lid and wait for it to cool before moving to step 6 and pitching (adding) the yeast. If the wort is too hot, you could kill off the yeast cells.

6 **Open the packet of yeast** and sprinkle it evenly over the surface of the wort. Check the instructions and, if required, add any sachets of hops or fruit. Close the lid of the fermenter, fit an airlock (if using), and leave to ferment.

⟫⟫ **See pp64–65 for more about fermentation** ⟫⟫

Using malt extract

Malt-extract brewing takes a little more time than using a kit (see pp54–55), but the use of fresh hops and speciality grains helps to create a fuller-flavoured, more aromatic beer.

Many people start their brewing career using the malt-extract method. This involves boiling un-hopped malt extract with hops. The key to making great beer is always to use very fresh ingredients.

The malt-extract recipes in this book use dried malt extract, which dissolves readily in cold water; liquid malt extract, if you decide to use it, dissolves better in hot water.

HOW MUCH WORT TO BOIL?

It is best to boil the total volume of wort (27 litres/47½ pints) if you can. However, if you prefer to boil a smaller volume, use 10 litres (17½ pints) of water and just 1kg (2¼lb) of dried malt extract. This will keep the gravity of the wort low – as it would have been if you had boiled the total volume – and so allow the hops to impart the correct level of bitterness. Ten minutes before the end of the boil, add the balance of malt extract, and top up the fermenter with cold water when ready.

EQUIPMENT

- Weighing scales
- Boiler or large pan
- Thermometer
- Grain bag (optional)
- Brewer's spoon or paddle
- Chiller (optional)
- Fermenter
- Hydrometer and trial jar
- Airlock (optional)

INGREDIENTS

- Malt extract (dried or liquid)
- Speciality grains (optional)
- Hops

PREPARATION ⏱ 30 MINS

Dried malt extract

Amber malt

Crystal malt

Chocolate malt

Protofloc

Hops

Hops

If adding grains, use a thermometer to take the temperature of the water

1 Planning is key for a successful brew day, so create a worksheet detailing every grain and hop addition. Make sure all your equipment is sterilized (see pp44–45), then weigh out each grain and hop addition.

2 Measure the required volume of water into a boiler or large pan, and turn on the heat. If the recipe calls for steeped grains, heat the water to 70°C (160°F). If not, bring the water to a boil and jump to step 4, opposite.

Using a grain bag makes it easier to remove the grains later on

Watch the pan closely as you boil the malt extract – in case the wort boils over

3 **Add the grains** to the water (use a grain bag if you have one). Close the boiler or pan lid and leave to infuse for 30 minutes. Keep the temperature at 65–70°C (149–160°F). Strain the grains (or remove the bag) and bring the water to a boil.

4 **Once the water is boiling,** remove the pan from the heat and add the malt extract (if using dried, dissolve it in a little cold water first). Stir well to remove any lumps, then bring the wort to a vigorous boil.

Allow the wort to cool a little before adding any aroma hops

5 **Add the first batch of hops** (for bittering) and set a timer to remind you when to make subsequent hop additions (for flavour). Add any aroma hops at the end of the boil, but only once the wort has cooled to 80°C (175°F).

6 **Cool the wort quickly** using a chiller (see p61), if you have one, or by placing the pan in ice water. Once the wort has cooled to 20–24°C (68–75°F), transfer it to the fermenter, take a hydrometer reading, and pitch the yeast.

See pp62–63 for pitching the yeast »

GETTING STARTED USING MALT EXTRACT

Full-mash brewing

This advanced method requires the most equipment, skill, and knowledge, but is still achievable for the novice home brewer. There are three key stages – the mash, the sparge, and the boil.

STAGE 1 – THE MASH
The mash (see opposite) involves steeping malt in hot water (liquor) for 1 hour – although there is no harm in leaving it for longer. This dissolves the starches in the grains and converts them into fermentable sugars.

STAGE 2 – THE SPARGE
The sparge (see p60) involves rinsing the steeped grains to extract as many of the fermentable sugars as possible. The sweet wort obtained during the sparge is then transferred to the boiler.

STAGE 3 – THE BOIL
The boil (see p61) involves bringing the wort to a vigorous boil and adding hops at various intervals as required by the recipe. The boil should last for at least an hour, during which time the wort is sterilized and the hops impart the right amount of bitterness, flavour, and aroma.

EQUIPMENT
- Weighing scales
- Boiler
- Hot liquor tank (HLT) (optional)
- Mash tun
- Sparge arm and tubing
- Brewer's spoon or paddle
- Hydrometer and trial jar
- Airlock
- Chiller

INGREDIENTS
- Grains
- Hops
- Protofloc (or Irish moss)

PREPARATION ⏰ UP TO 1 HR

Pale malt

Amber malt

Flaked maize

Hops

Protofloc

1 **Add the total liquor** to the boiler or HLT and heat to 77°C (171°F). This may take up to 1 hour, depending on your boiler. For convenience, and if using an HLT with a timer, set it to come on before the start of your brew day.

2 **Prepare ahead** for a stress-free brew day. Weigh out the ingredients in advance, including any protofloc (or Irish moss, if using), and label each hop addition and time. Add some hot liquor to the mash tun to warm it up.

Stage 1 – The mash

The ideal temperature for the mash is 65–68°C (149–154°F). The high end of this range produces less fermentable sugars – for sweeter, weaker beers; the low end produces more fermentable sugars – for drier, stronger beers. Use 2.5 litres (4½ pints) of hot water per 1kg (2¼lb) of grain. This will allow you to add extra hot or cold water to adjust the temperature as needed.

THREE MAIN TYPES OF MASH

■ Single-stage infusion mashing (see below) involves holding the temperature constant for the duration of the mash. This is the simplest and most popular method among both commercial and home brewers.

■ Multi-rest mashing involves starting the mash at a low temperature, before raising and holding the temperature, and then raising and holding it again. This increases the sugar yield from the malt.

■ Decoction mashing involves raising the temperature in stages by removing a portion of grain, boiling it separately, and then returning it to the main mash. This can be done in 1, 2, or 3 stages (single-, double-, or triple-decoction mashing) and produces extra malt characters.

STUCK MASH

Be careful not to over-stir the grains as you combine them in the mash tun – this can cause a "stuck" mash. A stuck mash is when the run-off during the sparge is very slow, or when the mash tap becomes completely blocked, making it impossible to transfer the wort to the boiler. If this happens, gently stir the grain to agitate it and then leave it to settle. Don't worry if the additional time needed to do this means the grains are in the mash tun for more than 1 hour, as it will not affect the character of the final brew.

SINGLE-STAGE INFUSION MASHING ⏱ APPROX 1 HR

3 Add the hot liquor and the grains to the mash tun – this is known as "doughing-in". Add the required liquor via the tap on the boiler or HLT, then pour in the grains very slowly to avoid creating lumps or dry areas.

4 Break up any lumps by slicing the mash in a gentle side-to-side motion using a spoon. Do not over-stir. Close the lid and leave for 1 hour. Meanwhile, check that the liquor left in your boiler or HLT is still at 77°C (171°F).

See pp60–61 for the sparge and boil

Stage 2 – The sparge

Once the grains have infused you will need to rinse the fermentable sugars from the mash and run the wort into the boiler. This is known as sparging. The water for sparging should be between 74–77°C (165–171°F) – any higher, and tannins from the grains will be dissolved, creating harsh, astringent flavours; any lower, and the run-off will be less fluid and fewer sugars will be extracted. Prepare at least 20 litres (35 pints) of sparge water.

THREE MAIN SPARGING METHODS

▧ Continuous sparging (see below) extracts the most amount of sugar from the grains. It involves adding a spray of water to the surface of the grains while draining an equal volume of wort from the bottom of the tun.

▧ Batch sparging involves adding hot water to the mash, stirring, and leaving to infuse for 20 minutes. A run-off is then taken and returned to the mash to filter any grain debris. When the run-off is clear, the wort is drained into the boiler and the process repeated.

▧ With the no-sparge method, the wort is run directly into the boiler. Although this is the easiest method, a lot of sugar will be left behind.

OVER SPARGING

Be careful not to over sparge. If your runnings drop below a specific gravity of 1010 when you take a reading, it means there is a likelihood that tannins are starting to be extracted from the grain. This will affect the quality of the finished beer.

To check the gravity of hot wort, add a drop or two to a refractometer (see p53) if you have one. This will automatically adjust for the high temperature.

CONTINUOUS SPARGING ⏱ 30–40 MINS

5 **Collect a run-off** from the mash tap and pour it back over the grain, repeating until the wort runs clear. Set up the sparge arm and connect it to the hot liquor tank (HLT) with tubing. Run a second tube from the mash tap to the boiler.

6 **Open the HLT tap** to begin sparging. Now open the mash tap to run hot wort into the bottom of the boiler, taking care not to splash the wort. Continue sparging until your boiler contains about 27 litres (47½ pints) of wort.

Stage 3 – The boil

With your boiler now containing the correct volume of wort, bring the brew to a rolling boil and add the hops according to the recipe. During the boil, alpha acids, flavours, and aromas are extracted from the hops (see pp28–30 for more about hops). The boil also sanitizes the wort, concentrates it, and helps get rid of unwanted proteins (see right).

COOLING THE WORT

■ At the end of the boil, you will need to cool the wort as quickly as possible to the correct temperature for pitching the yeast. A rapid cool prevents the wort from being contaminated, and doesn't hold up your brew day. The most effective way to cool the wort at the end of the boil is to use an immersion chiller (see p51 and step 8, below). This will cool the wort to fermentation temperature (20°C/68°F) in about 20 minutes. Sterilize the chiller by placing it in the boiler for the last 10 minutes of the boil.

■ If you don't have a chiller – and are not using a boiler with an electric element – you can place the boiler in a bath of ice-cold water. This is the easiest method, but it will take at least an hour to cool a full batch of wort.

THE HOT AND COLD BREAK
The high temperature of the rolling boil will create a "hot break" and the rapid reduction in temperature when cooling will create a "cold break". This occurs when proteins in the wort are forced out of suspension in the liquid, coagulate, and then drop to the bottom of the boiler. These breaks prevent proteins from being transferred to the fermenter, which can cause "chill haze" in the finished beer.

BOILING AND COOLING THE WORT ⏰ 1 HR 30 MINS – 2 HRS

7 Bring the wort to a rolling boil and wait for the hot break before adding the first batch of hops (for bittering). Then follow the boil schedule in the recipe, adding hops (for flavour and aroma) as directed.

Be careful – the output water from the chiller can be very hot

8 Lower the chiller into the wort towards the end of the boil. When ready, flow cold water slowly through it. When the wort reaches 20–22°C (68–72°F), transfer it to the fermenter, fully opening the boiler tap to oxygenate the wort.

See pp62–63 for pitching the yeast

Pitching the yeast

Regardless of how the wort is produced, all home brewers must pitch, or add, yeast to start fermentation. After a few days, your recipe may require more hops. This is known as dry hopping.

Pitching the correct level, or amount, of yeast is key to healthy fermentation. Under pitching will put strain on the yeast, lengthen the lag time (see p64), and increase the chances of infection. Over pitching can introduce unwanted flavours and decrease head retention. The level of yeast required depends on the volume, gravity, and temperature:

- One packet of dried yeast is enough to ferment 23 litres (40 pints).
- Higher gravity beers (those over 1060) contain more fermentable sugars and require more yeast. Use 2 packets per batch.
- Use 2 packets per batch when fermenting at lower temperatures.

YEAST STARTERS
A liquid-yeast starter is a solution of liquid yeast, dried malt extract (DME), and water that is allowed to ferment. The aim is to propagate the yeast cells prior to pitching for improved fermentation. See p213 for details of online calculators to help you determine the required starter volume.

DRIED VS LIQUID YEAST
Dried yeast keeps well and can be sprinkled directly over the wort. As long as it is within its use-by date and stored in a cool place, it should contain enough live cells to ferment a typical batch of beer.

In contrast, the number of live cells in liquid yeast decreases over time. Most must be used within 4 months, but the older they are, the less viable the yeast will be. A typical liquid yeast contains enough live cells to ferment just 18 litres (31½ pints), so it is best to use a yeast starter (see below).

MAKING A LIQUID-YEAST STARTER ⏱ 15 MINS, PLUS 2 DAYS' FERMENTATION

1 **Find a vessel that holds** 1 litre (1¾ pints) more than the starter volume. An Erlenmeyer, or conical, flask is ideal as you can use it to both boil and chill the starter. Dissolve the DME (100g/3½oz for a 1-litre/1¾-pint starter) in water.

2 **Top up the flask** with water to the required volume and bring to a boil. After 15 minutes, remove from the heat and cool in ice water (if not using a flask, boil the starter in a pan, then add the cooled wort to a sterilized vessel).

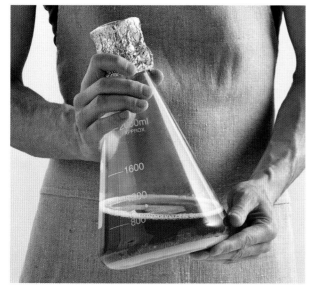

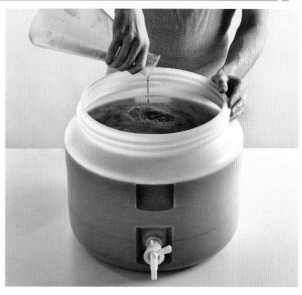

3 **Add the yeast** then cover the flask or vessel with silver foil and shake well. Leave for about 2 days, periodically shaking to introduce plenty of oxygen. Once fermentation is complete, allow the yeast sediment to settle.

4 **Pour off and discard** all the liquid before pitching the yeast. Once the wort in your fermenter has cooled to 20–24°C (68–75°F) add the yeast sediment, close the fermenter lid, and add an airlock (if using).

DRY HOPPING

Dry hopping involves adding fresh hops to the fermenter a few days after pitching the yeast – once primary fermentation (see p64) is complete. Dry hopping has the benefit of introducing powerful hop aromas from a relatively small amount of hops. This is because the aromas and essential oils are not driven off, either by the heat of the boil or by the carbon dioxide produced during primary fermentation.

■ Dry hop about 4 days after pitching the yeast, when alcohol will be present in the beer – alcohol will kill off any bacteria from the hops – and very little carbon dioxide is being produced.

■ Use a hop bag to avoid particles being transferred to the finished beer. A bag also makes removing the hops far easier.

■ Remove the dry hops after about 1 week. Any longer and they may introduce an unwanted, grassy character to the beer.

■ Use 25–50g (scant 1–1¾oz) for a typical batch, although this will depend on the strength of the particular hop variety – feel free to experiment.

■ Dry hops can be added to beers created using a kit, malt extract, or the full-mash method.

FINING AGENTS

Finings are added during the brewing process to help clarify the beer. They cause particles suspended in the liquid to clump together and sink to the bottom of the fermenter, where they are less likely to be transferred to the finished beer. Finings are added at 2 key stages:

■ During the last 10–15 minutes of the boil, when they are known as copper finings (the "copper" being the traditional name for the boiler). Copper finings, such as protofloc and Irish moss, prevent proteins from the malt being transferred to the fermenter and are highly recommended.

■ After fermentation is complete, to speed up the final stage of clearing. Commercial brewers add finings to decrease the time taken for the beer to settle after transportation. For home brewers, however, it comes down to personal choice as gravity will clear your beer in time. Isinglass, produced from the swim bladders of fish, is a popular choice.

The fermentation process

Once you have produced a wort and pitched the yeast, the next stage of the brewing process is fermentation – when the sweet, non-alcoholic liquid is transformed into beer.

THREE KEY STAGES OF FERMENTATION

■ The first stage of fermentation is the lag or adaptive phase, when the yeast cells start to multiply. The wort is easily contaminated at this point, so the shorter the lag, the better – ideally no more than 24 hours. After this time, a cream-coloured head, or krausen, should form.

■ The second stage is the primary or attenuative phase – when the yeast ferments the sugars in the wort and produces, among other things, alcohol and carbon dioxide. This usually takes a few days, during which time the gravity will decrease and the krausen will subside. It is normal to notice a dirty residue, floating particles, and even a pungent smell at this point.

■ Finally, there is the secondary or conditioning phase, when the yeast removes any unwanted by-products (natural chemical compounds such as esters and diacetyl). This helps create a clear, clean-tasting beer.

OXYGEN AND TEMPERATURE

During the lag phase, the presence of oxygen is crucial – without it, the yeast cells would be unable to multiply effectively. For the home brewer, lots of splashing and stirring just before pitching the yeast should be enough to introduce the required amount of oxygen. It is important to note, however, that this is the only time during the whole brewing process when oxygen should be introduced.

Keeping the wort at the correct temperature will promote healthy yeast growth and provide a suitable environment for fermentation. Each yeast strain performs best within a particular temperature range, and by working within this range a brewer can modify the final taste of the beer. Lower temperatures usually result in cleaner-tasting beers, while warmer temperatures tend to produce additional flavour compounds – either outcome may be desirable.

As your beer ferments, a dirty residue may form around the sides of the fermenter

---

TIPS FOR HEALTHY FERMENTATION

■ Before pitching the yeast, make sure plenty of oxygen has been introduced to the wort. You can do this by splashing the cooled wort into the fermenter after the boil and then stirring vigorously.

■ To help kick-start fermentation, always begin at a slightly higher temperature than stated in the recipe. You can then decrease the temperature when signs of fermentation are visible.

■ Always pitch the correct amount of healthy yeast – too little, and fermentation may stall; too much, and off-flavours may be introduced (see p62 for pitching levels).

1 **Taking a gravity reading** using a hydrometer is the only accurate way of knowing when fermentation is complete (when the reading matches the expected final gravity). To do this, first take a sample of wort using a sterilized trial jar.

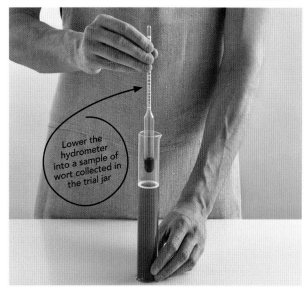

Lower the hydrometer into a sample of wort collected in the trial jar

2 **Holding the hydrometer** at the top of the stem, lower it into the sample. When the hydrometer reaches its point of equilibrium, carefully let go, then wait for it to settle. If bubbles are obscuring the scale, gently turn the stem to release them.

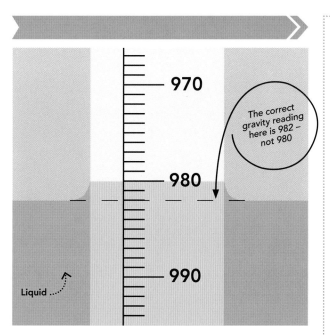

970

The correct gravity reading here is 982 – not 980

980

990

Liquid

3 **Take the reading** at eye level, reading the scale at the same plane as the horizontal surface of the liquid – not at the point where the liquid rises up as it touches the stem of the hydrometer.

HOW TO CALCULATE ABV

As well as indicating when fermentation is complete, gravity readings can be used to calculate how much sugar has been converted to alcohol, and so determine the strength of your brew. You will need to take a reading before pitching the yeast (the original gravity or OG) and a second reading before bottling or barrelling (the final gravity or FG). Multiplying the difference between these two readings by 105 will give you the percentage of alcohol by weight. To determine the percentage of alcohol by volume (ABV) – the measure used by most commercial brewers – simply multiply the alcohol-by-weight figure by 1.25. So, for example:

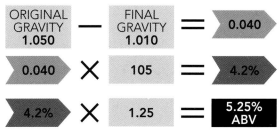

ORIGINAL GRAVITY 1.050	−	FINAL GRAVITY 1.010	=	0.040
0.040	×	105	=	4.2%
4.2%	×	1.25	=	5.25% ABV

GETTING STARTED THE FERMENTATION PROCESS

Priming and racking

For a beer to achieve the right level of carbonation when served, it needs to be primed with sugar. Priming is done just before the beer is transferred to bottles or barrels – a process known as racking.

Beers such as lager and wheat beer are best served highly carbonated and with a large head. Ales, which appear quite flat, still require the right amount of carbon dioxide (CO_2) to produce a small head and a slight tingle on the tongue. To carbonate your beer, you will need to add a small amount of fermentable sugar prior to racking.

CALCULATING PRIMING SUGAR QUANTITIES

The amount of sugar needed depends on the type of sugar being used, the size of the batch of beer, and the desired level of carbonation. The most common sugars are corn (or brewing) sugar, cane sugar, and dried malt extract (DME). The chart below shows the level of carbon dioxide required for each beer style (shown as a ratio of volumes of CO_2 per volume of beer) and the amount of sugar needed to achieve this level of carbonation. It assumes a storing temperature of 20°C (68°F).

PRIMING SOLUTION

The best way to prime your beer is to make a solution by dissolving the sugar or DME in a little boiling water. Allow it to cool, add it to the fermenter, and then stir gently with a sterilized spoon, taking care not to disturb the sediment.

Making a solution will help evenly distribute the sugar. The method is also more accurate than adding sugar directly to each bottle. This is important, as an over-primed bottle is at risk of exploding.

CARBONATION PRIMING CHART

BEER STYLE	CO_2 (Volumes of CO_2 per volume of beer)	CORN SUGAR (Weight required per volume of beer)	CANE SUGAR (Weight required per volume of beer)	DME (Weight required per volume of beer)
Light lagers, bock, pale ale, and fruit beers	2.5	7.4g per litre (0.15oz per pint)	6.5g per litre (0.13oz per pint)	8.4g per litre (0.17oz per pint)
Amber lager; light and amber hybrids	2.4	7g per litre (0.14oz per pint)	6.1g per litre (0.12oz per pint)	7.9g per litre (0.16oz per pint)
Dark lager	2.6	7.9g per litre (0.16oz per pint)	6.9g per litre (0.14oz per pint)	8.9g per litre (0.18oz per pint)
IPA, mild; herb and spice beers	2	5.1g per litre (0.1oz per pint)	4.5g per litre (0.09oz per pint)	5.8g per litre (0.12oz per pint)
Sour and lambic ales; wheat and rye beers	3.75	13.2g per litre (0.26oz per pint)	11.5g per litre (0.23oz per pint)	14.9g per litre (0.3oz per pint)
Bitter	1.5	2.8g per litre (0.06oz per pint)	2.5g per litre (0.05oz per pint)	3.2g per litre (0.06oz per pint)
Strong ale	1.9	4.7g per litre (0.09oz per pint)	4.1g per litre (0.08oz per pint)	5.3g per litre (0.11oz per pint)
Brown ale	1.75	4g per litre (0.08oz per pint)	3.5g per litre (0.07oz per pint)	4.5g per litre (0.09oz per pint)
Barley wine	1.8	4.2g per litre (0.08oz per pint)	3.7g per litre (0.07oz per pint)	4.8g per litre (0.1oz per pint)
Stout and porter	2	5.1g per litre (0.1oz per pint)	4.5g per litre (0.09oz per pint)	5.8g per litre (0.12oz per pint)

RACKING YOUR BEER

Transferring your beer from one vessel to another is known as racking. This may be to another fermenter for extended conditioning in a separate, clean vessel, or to bottles or barrels for storage.

If your fermenter has a tap, simply connect a length of tubing, place the open end of the tube into the desired receptacle, and turn on the tap. If it doesn't have tap, feed the tubing into the top of the fermenter and siphon the beer. As you siphon, take care not to disturb the yeast sediment at the bottom of the fermenter as you don't want this to be transferred as well (some siphons have a sediment trap to help prevent this – see p49).

Avoid splashing

Racking must be carried out as carefully as possible, with the minimum of splashing. Splashing will introduce oxygen, which can spoil the flavour of the finished beer and introduce unwanted bacteria. To avoid unnecessary splashing when racking, place the open end of the tubing right at the bottom of the receiving container, and then submerge it once enough beer has been transferred.

1 **Clean each bottle** with a bottle brush to remove any debris, especially yeast sediment from previous brews that may have collected at the bottom. Then sterilize and rinse the bottles.

2 **Connect one end** of a plastic tube to the fermenter tap and the other to a bottle-filling stick. Place the stick inside a bottle, turn on the tap, and press down to release the valve and start the flow. Repeat for each bottle.

Before you start, double check that you have enough bottles and caps for the whole batch

3 **To cap the bottles,** slot a crown cap into the bottle capper and position it over the neck of the first filled bottle. Using two hands, firmly push down the levers. Remove the capper and repeat for each bottle.

GETTING STARTED PRIMING AND RACKING

Storing and serving

Before you can sample your brew, it needs to be left to condition in a suitable container. This allows the beer to clear and lets the flavours mature. There are several storage options available.

PRESSURE BARRELS

These are typically large plastic containers designed to withstand pressure up to about 41kPa (6 psi). If the pressure exceeds this, a valve in the top allows the brew to vent, preventing possible explosions. Most types of pressure barrel hold up to 25 litres (44 pints) of beer. Priming sugar is added to the beer prior to barrelling (see p66) and, as the beer is drunk and the pressure naturally decreases, additional CO_2 can be added via a valve.

ADVANTAGES

- Inexpensive
- Easy to clean and sterilize
- Quick and easy to transfer beer from fermenter when racking
- Beer will keep for many months
- Usually fitted with a tap, so no additional equipment required for serving

DISADVANTAGES

- May need to be stored in a cool area or fridge to serve beer at the right temperature
- It can be difficult to maintain the correct level of carbonation
- There can be some wastage due to dead space below the tap

Plastic pressure barrel

KEGS AND CASKS

A keg is a large container for storing and dispensing beer under pressure. It can be connected to a separate CO_2 supply. The most popular type is the stainless steel Cornelius keg (see left), which holds 19 litres (33 pints). It can withstand pressure up to 965kPa (140 psi) so highly carbonated beers can be served.

Casks, used by most commercial brewers, are made of metal or plastic and come in several sizes – commonly the 40-litre (70-pint) "firkin". Unlike other containers they let in oxygen, which adds an authentic real-ale character to the beer but means it quickly goes stale. Home brewers may need to connect a CO_2 bottle.

Cornelius keg

ADVANTAGES OF KEGS

- Durable and easy to clean, sterilize, store, and refrigerate.
- Allow you to control the level of carbonation and are great for serving highly carbonated beers
- No priming sugar needs to be added, resulting in less sediment and a shorter conditioning time
- Beer will keep for many months
- Limited wastage as beer is drawn from the bottom of the keg

DISADVANTAGES OF KEGS

- Expensive initial set-up
- More complicated to use
- May need to be stored in a cool area or fridge to serve beer at the right temperature

BOTTLES

For many home brewers, bottles are the best way to store beer. Available in several sizes and in plastic or glass, they can be refrigerated and are easy to transport. Most require you to add a crown or screw cap, although some have a convenient swing-top stopper. Bottles do, however, take a long time to clean, sterilize, and fill, and will result in high carbonation levels (which is great for lagers and wheat beers but not so good for ales). Avoid using clear bottles as sunlight will react with the hops and cause off-flavours.

ADVANTAGES
- Easy to store in the fridge
- Easy to transport and ideal for giving as gifts
- Beer will keep for many months

DISADVANTAGES
- Time-consuming to prepare and fill
- Better suited for beers served with high levels of carbonation

SERVING BEER FROM A BOTTLE ⏰ 1 MIN

1 **Select a clean glass** and make sure the beer is at the right temperature (9–12°C/48–54°F for ales; lagers should be chilled). Hold the glass at an angle of about 45° and pour slowly in one smooth motion.

2 **Straighten the glass** slowly to allow the head to develop. The bottle may contain yeast sediment, so be careful not to transfer this to the glass (although you may wish to rouse the yeast for styles served hazy – such as wheat beers).

Labelling bottles

If you are storing your brew in bottles, you can personalize your beer by creating your own labels. Not only is this fun, but it also produces a professional-looking final product.

Creating a label will allow you identify each brew so you always know what you are drinking. You can also create an identity that suits the style of beer and reflects your own personality – ideal if you intend to give bottles away as gifts or are brewing a batch of beer for a special occasion.

DESIGN CONSIDERATIONS

■ Decide on a shape for your label – roundels, ovals, and shields, for example, are all classic shapes.

■ Include a main image – you could use design software, scan a hand-drawn sketch, or import a photograph.

■ Pick a font for the text, and add the name of your beer, the style, alcohol content, volume, and any other description.

■ Don't worry if your design skills are lacking as there are several label generators online (see p213). Most allow you to add your own details to a series of generic templates.

■ Finally, print them on plain white paper using a laser printer.

Name of brew *Style of beer*

GOLDEN RAM WEIZEN BOCK

3.7% ABV   500ml
BREWED IN DORSET BY GEOFF PETERS

Alcohol content   *Volume*
Additional information

LABEL GALLERY

Look out for these sample labels, which accompany some of the recipes in the book. You could use them as inspiration for your own designs and add the extra information as suggested above.

EUROPEAN LAGER — See p83

JAPANESE RICE LAGER — See p89

DOPPELBOCK — See p102

HARVEST **PALE ALE** — See p114

Northern Brown Ale — See p160

MILD — See p164

DRY STOUT — See p174

AMERICAN STOUT — See p177

WEIZEN BOCK — See p184

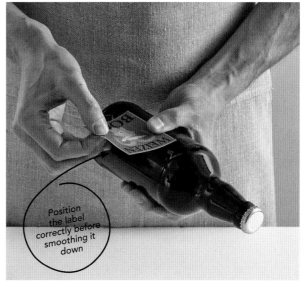

Position the label correctly before smoothing it down

1 **Using a small paint brush** or pastry brush, apply a thin coat of milk to the back of the label. Milk is great as an adhesive as it sticks well but enables labels to be easily soaked off for future batches (and it doesn't smell!).

2 **Holding a bottle** in one hand, carefully position the label with your other hand. Make any alignment adjustments, and then smooth the label around the bottle, wiping off any drips of milk with a dry cloth.

Honey Ale — See p124

American IPA — See p133

60 SHILLING — See p145

IRISH RED ALE — See p149

Abbey BEER — See p154

Roggenbier — See p188

DARK WHEAT BEER — See p193

Cream Ale — See p196

CALIFORNIAN Common — See p198

NETTLE BEER — See p211

Beer styles and recipes

Recipe choosers

Whether you are a dedicated "hop head" or prefer rich, full-bodied beers, use these recipe choosers to find the right beer for you. You'll find all these recipes, and lots more, on pp80–211.

Fruity and zingy beers

- **Munich Helles** (see p85)
- **Oktoberfest** (see p98)
- **Spring Beer** (see p112)
- **Heather Ale** (see p125)
- **Cherry Lambic** (see pp138–39)
- **Abbey Beer** (see p154)
- **Roggenbier** (see p188)
- **Spiced Honey Beer** (see p204)
- **Spruce beer** (see p203)

- **Raspberry Wheat Beer** (see pp206–07)
- **Strawberry Beer** (see p208)
- **Kiwi Witbier** (see p209)

- **Ginger Beer** (see p205)
- **Spiced Coriander and Lime Beer** (see p202)
- **Nettle Beer** (see p211)

Raspberry Wheat Beer (see pp206–07) **Cherry Lambic** (see pp138–39)

Crisp and refreshing beers

- **Light Lager** (see p82)
- **European Lager** (see p83)
- **Mexican Cerveza** (see p88)
- **Japanese Rice Lager** (see p89)
- **Czech Pilsner** (see pp90–91)
- **Bohemian Pilsner** (see p94)
- **American Pilsner** (see p95)
- **Vienna Lager** (see pp96–97)
- **Helles Bock** (see p99)
- **Black Lager** (see p107)
- **Elderflower Ale** (see p113)
- **East Kent Golding Single Hop Ale** (see p119)
- **Saaz Single Hop Ale** (see p120)
- **English IPA** (see p131)
- **Summer Ale** (see pp142–43)
- **Weissbier** (see p185)
- **American Wheat Beer** (see pp186–87)
- **Witbier** (see pp190–91)
- **Kölsch** (see p197)
- **Raspberry Wheat Beer** (see pp206–07)

Witbier (see pp190–91)

Summer Ale (see pp142–43)

Vienna Lager (see pp96–97)

Amarillo Single Hop Ale (see pp116–17)

Dark American Lager (see pp104–05)

Bière de Garde (see pp152–53)

Hoppy beers

- **Amarillo Single Hop Ale** (see pp116–17)
- **Nelson Sauvin Single Hop Ale** (see p118)
- **Cascade Single Hop Ale** (see p121)
- **60-Minute IPA** (see p132)
- **American IPA** (see p133)
- **Imperial IPA** (see pp134–35)
- **Black IPA** (see p136)
- **Rye Beer** (see p189)

Rich and full-bodied beers

- **Traditional Bock** (see pp100–01)
- **Doppelbock** (see p102)
- **Eisbock** (see p103)
- **Dark American Lager** (see pp104–05)
- **Munich Dunkel** (see p106)
- **ESB** (see p115)
- **Saison** (see p127)
- **Smoked Beer** (see p130)
- **London Bitter** (see p140)
- **Yorkshire Bitter** (see p141)
- **Cornish Tin Miner's Ale** (see p144)

- **Scottish 70 Shilling**
  (see pp146–47)

- **Scottish 80 Shilling**
  (see p148)

- **Irish Red Ale** (see p149)

- **Winter Warmer** (see p150)

- **Christmas Ale** (see p151)

- **Bière de Garde**
  (see pp152–53)

- **Belgian Dubbel**
  (see p156)

- **Belgian Tripel** (see p157)

- **Belgian Strong Golden Ale** (see pp158–59)

- **Northern Brown Ale**
  (see p160)

- **Southern Brown Ale**
  (see p161)

- **Old Ale** (see pp162–63)

- **Mild** (see p164)

- **Ruby Mild** (see p165)

- **English Barley Wine**
  (see pp166–67)

- **American Barley Wine**
  (see p168)

- **Brown Porter** (see p169)

- **Smoked Porter** (see p170)

- **American Stout** (see p177)

- **Milk Stout** (see p178)

- **Russian Imperial Stout**
  (see p180)

- **Vanilla Bourbon Stout**
  (see p181)

Old Ale (see pp162–63)

Scottish 70 Shilling (see pp146–47)

How to use the recipes

The recipes in the book are all designed for full-mash brewing, although many have malt extract versions, too. See below for information about each part of the recipe.

KEY INFORMATION

Original gravity (OG) – the density of the wort prior to fermentation, as read on a hydrometer (see p49 and p65).

Expected final gravity (FG) – the density of the wort once fermentation is complete.

Total liquor – the total amount of water required to produce the batch.

BREWING ICONS

Makes – the expected final volume of beer that will be produced.

Ready to drink – the earliest the beer will be ready to consume, although most styles improve with extended ageing.

Estimated ABV – the estimated alcoholic strength of the final beer.

Bitterness rating – how bitter the beer will taste; the higher the number, the more bitter it will be (although a high ABV will balance out a high bitterness).

Colour rating – how light or dark the beer will be, measured on the EBC scale (see pp22–23); the higher the number, the darker the beer.

MALT EXTRACT VERSION

Follow these instructions if you want to use malt extract (see pp56–57) instead of the full-mash method (see pp58–61). It assumes you will be boiling 27 litres (47½ pints) of water in a large pan. If you wish to work with a smaller volume, boil 10 litres (17½ pints) of water, adding 1kg (2¼lb) of dried malt extra at the start of the boil. Add the balance of malt extract in the last 5 minutes.

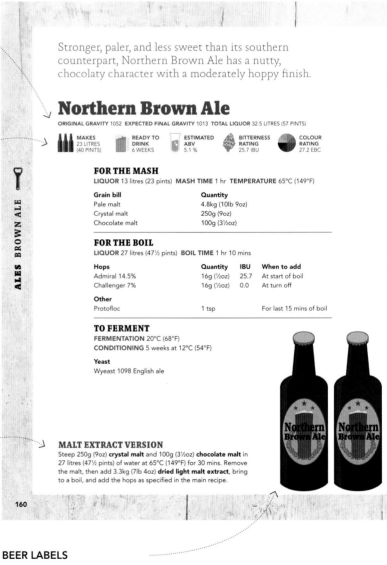

Stronger, paler, and less sweet than its southern counterpart, Northern Brown Ale has a nutty, chocolaty character with a moderately hoppy finish.

Northern Brown Ale

ORIGINAL GRAVITY 1052 EXPECTED FINAL GRAVITY 1013 TOTAL LIQUOR 32.5 LITRES (57 PINTS)

MAKES 23 LITRES (40 PINTS)	**READY TO DRINK** 6 WEEKS	**ESTIMATED ABV** 5.1 %	**BITTERNESS RATING** 25.7 IBU **COLOUR RATING** 27.2 EBC

FOR THE MASH
LIQUOR 13 litres (23 pints) MASH TIME 1 hr TEMPERATURE 65°C (149°F)

Grain bill	Quantity
Pale malt	4.8kg (10lb 9oz)
Crystal malt	250g (9oz)
Chocolate malt	100g (3½oz)

FOR THE BOIL
LIQUOR 27 litres (47½ pints) BOIL TIME 1 hr 10 mins

Hops	Quantity	IBU	When to add
Admiral 14.5%	16g (½oz)	25.7	At start of boil
Challenger 7%	16g (½oz)	0.0	At turn off

Other		
Protofloc	1 tsp	For last 15 mins of boil

TO FERMENT
FERMENTATION 20°C (68°F)
CONDITIONING 5 weeks at 12°C (54°F)

Yeast
Wyeast 1098 English ale

MALT EXTRACT VERSION
Steep 250g (9oz) **crystal malt** and 100g (3½oz) **chocolate malt** in 27 litres (47½ pints) of water at 65°C (149°F) for 30 mins. Remove the malt, then add 3.3kg (7lb 4oz) **dried light malt extract**, bring to a boil, and add the hops as specified in the main recipe.

160

ALES BROWN ALE

BEER LABELS

Use these sample labels as a starting point for your own designs. See pp70–71 for more about labelling bottles.

QUICK BREW

This symbol indicates, at a glance, which beers will be ready to drink the soonest.

FOR THE MASH

Liquor – the water required for mixing with the grains in the mash tun. Use the balance of the "total liquor" (see opposite) for sparging.

Mash time – the minimum time required for the mash (although there is no harm in leaving it for longer).

Temperature – the required temperature for the mash, once the grains and water have been combined.

Grain bill – the type and quantity of crushed grains required for the mash.

Also known as London ale, this style originated in the early 20th century as an alternative to porter and mild. Moderately low in alcohol, it has a sweet, malty finish.

QUICK BREW

Southern Brown Ale

ORIGINAL GRAVITY 1041 EXPECTED FINAL GRAVITY 1012 TOTAL LIQUOR 31 LITRES (54½ PINTS)

MAKES 23 LITRES (40 PINTS)	**READY TO DRINK** 4 WEEKS	**ESTIMATED ABV** 3.8%	**BITTERNESS RATING** 17.4 IBU	**COLOUR RATING** 37.6 EBC

FOR THE MASH

LIQUOR 10 litres (17½ pints) MASH TIME 1 hr TEMPERATURE 65°C (149°F)

Grain bill	Quantity
Pale malt	3.5kg (7lb 11oz)
Dark crystal malt	300g (10½oz)
Chocolate malt	110g (4oz)
Torrified wheat	100g (3½oz)
Black malt	55g (2oz)

FOR THE BOIL

LIQUOR 27 litres (47½ pints) BOIL TIME 1 hr 10 mins

Hops	Quantity	IBU	When to add
Fuggle 4.5%	24g (¾oz)	12.9	At start of boil
Fuggle 4.5%	24g (¾oz)	4.5	For last 10 mins of boil
Other			
Protofloc	1 tsp		For last 15 mins of boil

TO FERMENT

FERMENTATION 22°C (72°F) CONDITIONING 3 weeks at 12°C (54°F)

Yeast
Wyeast 1187 Ringwood ale

BREWER'S TIP
If you would prefer a slightly drier-tasting beer, try using Wyeast 1099 Whitbread ale instead of the Ringwood.

MALT EXTRACT VERSION
Steep 300g (10½oz) **dark crystal malt**, 110g (4oz) **chocolate malt**, and 55g (2oz) **black malt** in 27 litres (47½ pints) of water at 65°C (149°F) for 30 mins. Remove the malt, then add 2.3kg (5lb 1oz) **dried light malt extract**, bring to a boil, and add the hops as specified in the main recipe.

161

ALES BROWN ALE

FOR THE BOIL

Liquor – the estimated volume of water required for the boiler once the mash has been sparged.

Boil time – the total boil time.

Hops – the type and quantity of hops required for the boil, and when to make each addition.

Other – the type and quantity of any other ingredients required, and when to make each addition.

TO FERMENT

Fermentation – the optimum temperature for fermentation.

Conditioning – the optimum time and temperature at which the beer should be stored after fermentation, once it has been bottled or kegged.

Yeast – the suggested yeast strain. See pp62–63 for more about quantities and starters, and pp34–35 for alternative yeast strains.

A NOTE ON MEASUREMENTS

Volumes and weights are given in metric measurements, with imperial equivalents in brackets. See p213 for further conversion information.

BREWER'S TIP

These elements include practical hints and tips to help you as you brew, and suggest ingredient variations for altering the character of the finished beer.

Lagers

The most popular style of beer, lager is consumed in vast quantities around the world. Most nations produce their own variation of the style.

Lager is defined by the type of yeast used during the brewing process. Lager yeast (*Saccharomyces pastorianus*) is bottom fermenting, meaning that it settles to the bottom of the fermenter during fermentation. In contrast, most ale yeasts rise to the surface of the wort (see p108).

LOW TEMPERATURES

Lager yeast performs best at low fermentation temperatures, usually about 12°C (54°F). This is followed by an extended conditioning period, also at low temperatures, which is known as "lagering". The word lager comes from the German word *lagern* meaning "to store". The lagering process helps remove many of the flavour compounds produced during fermentation. The result is a clear, crisp-tasting beer with a neutral flavour and a clean finish. Usually there is little or no hop aroma, although there may be a subtle spiciness. Lager is best served cold and well carbonated.

HOME-BREW LAGER

For the home brewer, lager is one of the most challenging styles to produce well. Not only does it require controlled, cool fermentation conditions, but its subtle, clean character means that any unwanted flavours accidently introduced during the brewing process will be noticeable – however small. That said, it is still possible to brew great lagers by paying proper attention to the fermentation conditions, yeast pitching rates, and cleanliness. The most important factor is temperature control, so investing in a dedicated brew fridge would be a wise investment for the serious lager home-brewer.

Light lager

Light lagers have a low alcohol and calorie content, low malt flavour, and a crisp, dry, almost watery finish. They often contain maize or rice.

- **Appearance** Very pale and straw-like in colour.
- **Taste** Crisp and dry, often with very little flavour. A dry, corn-like sweetness is sometimes evident.
- **Aroma** A light, spicy hop aroma may be present, although there is often little or no apparent aroma.
- **Strength** 2.8–4.2% ABV
- (EU) European light lagers are low in alcohol. As they are brewed wholly with malt – and contain no maize or rice – they are usually more flavourful than their American counterparts.
- (US) American light lagers are very clean and light tasting with few key defining flavours.

See pp82–89

Pilsner

Originating from the Czech city of Plzeň (Pilsen), Pilsner is hoppier and has more complex malt flavours than other light lagers.

Appearance Light straw to deep gold in colour, with a lasting, creamy, white head.

Taste Has complex malty flavours and a soft bitterness, often with a slightly sweet finish.

Aroma Spicy, floral aromas mixed with a grainy, malt character.

Strength 4.2–6% ABV

(CZ) Czech Pilsners are lightly flavoured and highly carbonated.

(DE) German Pilsners have a fairly deep colour with a complex malt flavour and bitterness.

(US) American Pilsners are highly hopped, but also have a grainy character from the use of maize or corn.

See pp90–95

Amber lager

Toasted malt flavours and aromas dominate this German style, which is traditionally brewed in spring and aged over the summer in caves.

Appearance Dark gold to deep orange in colour, crystal clear, and with a lingering, off-white head.

Taste Deep, complex malt flavours are balanced by plenty of hop bitterness.

Aroma A lightly toasted, malty aroma, with little or no hop presence.

Strength 4.5–5.7% ABV

(EU) European versions are quite sweet, with complex malt flavours.

(US) American versions are stronger, drier, and have a more assertive hop character.

See pp96–98

Bock and dark lager

Bock is typically dark, strong, and sweet. Other dark lagers range from deep amber to pitch black.

Appearance Deep and intense with a creamy, off-white head.

Taste Bocks are smooth, rich, and caramel-like, with a low hop presence. Other dark lagers may have delicate, burnt flavour notes and a clean, dry, refreshing aftertaste.

Aroma Bocks have a strong toasted malt aroma with little or no hop aroma. Other dark lagers may have hints of chocolate, caramel, or nuts.

Strength 4.2–14% ABV, depending on the style.

(DE) There are several bock styles, all from Germany. Traditional bock is sweet, strong and mildly fruity. Doppelbock is dark, strong and bitter. Helles bock is paler, less malty, and hoppier.

See pp99–107

81

Pale straw in colour, crisp and refreshing on the palate, this clean-tasting lager is perfect when served chilled. The reduced alcohol content makes this a lower-calorie brew.

Light Lager

ORIGINAL GRAVITY 1038 **EXPECTED FINAL GRAVITY** 1011 **TOTAL LIQUOR** 30.7 LITRES (54 PINTS)

 MAKES 23 LITRES (40 PINTS)　 **READY TO DRINK** 5 WEEKS　 **ESTIMATED ABV** 3.4%　 **BITTERNESS RATING** 9.4 IBU　**COLOUR RATING** 5.5 EBC

FOR THE MASH

LIQUOR 9.3 litres (16 pints) **MASH TIME** 1 hr **TEMPERATURE** 65°C (149°F)

Grain bill	Quantity
Lager malt	2.81kg (6lb 3oz)
Flaked maize	939g (2lb 1oz)

FOR THE BOIL

LIQUOR 27 litres (47½ pints) **BOIL TIME** 1 hr 15 mins

Hops	Quantity	IBU	When to add
Hallertauer Hersbrucker 3.5%	20g (⅔oz)	8.5	At start of boil
Hallertauer Hersbrucker 3.5%	10g (⅓oz)	0.8	For last 5 mins of boil
Other			
Protofloc	1 tsp		For last 15 mins of boil

TO FERMENT

FERMENTATION 12°C (54°F) **CONDITIONING** 4 weeks at 3°C (37°F)

Yeast
Wyeast 2000 Budvar

BREWER'S TIP

When brewing lagers, it is best to use a large proportion of distilled or de-ionized water to help maintain the correct pH levels and avoid "off" flavours.

This golden European-style lager is smooth, full-bodied, and highly drinkable, with a delicious malty flavour and a crisp, clean finish.

European Lager

ORIGINAL GRAVITY 1045 **EXPECTED FINAL GRAVITY** 1015 **TOTAL LIQUOR** 34 LITRES (60 PINTS)

 MAKES 23 LITRES (40 PINTS)

 READY TO DRINK 5 WEEKS

 ESTIMATED ABV 4.6%

 BITTERNESS RATING 25.7 IBU

 COLOUR RATING 5.6 EBC

FOR THE MASH

LIQUOR 14 litres (24½ pints) **MASH TIME** 1 hr **TEMPERATURE** 65°C (149°F)

Grain bill	Quantity
Pilsner malt	3.95kg (8lb 11oz)
Flaked barley	400g (14oz)
Carapils malt	135g (4¾oz)

FOR THE BOIL

LIQUOR 27 litres (47½ pints) **BOIL TIME** 1 hr 15 mins

Hops	Quantity	IBU	When to add
Northern Brewer 8%	26g (1oz)	23.8	At start of boil
Hallertauer Hersbrucker 3.5%	12g (½oz)	1.7	For last 10 mins of boil
Hallertauer Hersbrucker 3.5%	15g (½oz)	0.1	For last 1 min of boil
Other			
Protofloc	1 tsp		For last 15 mins of boil

TO FERMENT

FERMENTATION 12°C (54°F) **CONDITIONING** 4 weeks at 3°C (37°F)

Yeast
Whitelabs WLP830 German lager

A classic American-style lager, this beer has a subtle hop aroma that is nicely balanced by a crisp, dry yeast profile and a mild bitterness.

Premium American Lager

ORIGINAL GRAVITY 1055 **EXPECTED FINAL GRAVITY** 1014 **TOTAL LIQUOR** 33 LITRES (58 PINTS)

 MAKES
23 LITRES
(40 PINTS)

 READY TO DRINK
5 WEEKS

 ESTIMATED ABV
5.5%

 BITTERNESS RATING
19 IBU

 COLOUR RATING
7.4 EBC

FOR THE MASH

LIQUOR 13 litres (23 pints) **MASH TIME** 1 hr **TEMPERATURE** 65°C (149°F)

Grain bill	Quantity
Lager malt	4.6kg (10lb 2oz)
Flaked rice	926g (2lb)

FOR THE BOIL

LIQUOR 27 litres (47½ pints) **BOIL TIME** 1 hr 15 mins

Hops	Quantity	IBU	When to add
Northern Brewer 8%	22g (¾oz)	18.8	At start of boil
Saaz 4.2%	11g (⅓oz)	0.2	For last 1 min of boil
Other			
Protofloc	1 tsp		For last 15 mins of boil

TO FERMENT

FERMENTATION 12°C (54°F) **CONDITIONING** 4 weeks at 3°C (37°F)

Yeast
Whitelabs WLP800 Pilsner

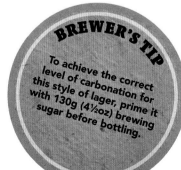

BREWER'S TIP
To achieve the correct level of carbonation for this style of lager, prime it with 130g (4½oz) brewing sugar before bottling.

Here, a slightly grainy, malty flavour – from the blend of lightly toasted malts – is balanced by the subtle bitterness and aroma of the spicy Mittelfrüh hops.

Munich Helles

ORIGINAL GRAVITY 1049 **EXPECTED FINAL GRAVITY** 1012 **TOTAL LIQUOR** 32 LITRES (56 PINTS)

 MAKES 23 LITRES (40 PINTS)

 READY TO DRINK 5 WEEKS

 ESTIMATED ABV 4.9%

 BITTERNESS RATING 17.1 IBU

 COLOUR RATING 6.3 EBC

FOR THE MASH

LIQUOR 12 litres (21 pints) **MASH TIME** 1 hr **TEMPERATURE** 65°C (149°F)

Grain bill	Quantity
Pilsner malt	4.38kg (9lb 10oz)
Carapils malt	200g (7oz)
Vienna malt	175g (6oz)

FOR THE BOIL

LIQUOR 27 litres (47½ pints) **BOIL TIME** 1 hr 15 mins

Hops	Quantity	IBU	When to add
Hallertauer Mittelfrüh 5%	27g (1oz)	14.9	At start of boil
Hallertauer Mittelfrüh 5%	20g (⅔oz)	2.2	For last 5 mins of boil

Other			
Protofloc	1 tsp		For last 15 mins of boil

TO FERMENT

FERMENTATION 12°C (54°F) **CONDITIONING** 4 weeks at 3°C (37°F)

Yeast
Wyeast 2042 Danish lager

This is a golden, slightly malty flavoured beer with a mild, spicy hop aroma. It finishes with a subtle sweetness and roundness in the mouth.

Dortmunder Export

ORIGINAL GRAVITY 1054 **EXPECTED FINAL GRAVITY** 1015 **TOTAL LIQUOR** 32.2 LITRES (56½ PINTS)

 MAKES 23 LITRES (40 PINTS)
 READY TO DRINK 5 WEEKS
 ESTIMATED ABV 5.1%
 BITTERNESS RATING 27.2 IBU
 COLOUR RATING 6 EBC

FOR THE MASH

LIQUOR 13.1 litres (23 pints) **MASH TIME** 1 hr **TEMPERATURE** 65°C (149°F)

Grain bill	Quantity
Pilsner malt	5kg (11lb)
Munich malt	250g (9oz)

FOR THE BOIL

LIQUOR 27 litres (47½ pints) **BOIL TIME** 1 hr 15 mins

Hops	Quantity	IBU	When to add
Tettnang 4.5%	40g (1⅓oz)	19.2	At start of boil
Hallertauer Hersbrucker 3.5%	26g (1oz)	3.5	For last 10 mins of boil
Tettnang 4.5%	26g (1oz)	4.5	For last 10 mins of boil
Hallertauer Hersbrucker 3.5%	13g (½oz)	0.0	At turn off

Other			
Protofloc	1 tsp		For last 15 mins of boil

TO FERMENT

FERMENTATION 12°C (54°F) **CONDITIONING** 4 weeks at 3°C (37°F)

Yeast
Wyeast 2124 Bohemian lager

Light, crisp, and refreshing, this Mexican-style beer is sure to hit the spot on a hot summer's day. Serve with a wedge of lime for an authentic flavour.

Mexican Cerveza

ORIGINAL GRAVITY 1046 **EXPECTED FINAL GRAVITY** 1012 **TOTAL LIQUOR** 31.5 LITRES (55½ PINTS)

 MAKES 23 LITRES (40 PINTS)   **READY TO DRINK** 5 WEEKS   **ESTIMATED ABV** 4.6%   **BITTERNESS RATING** 23.5 IBU   **COLOUR RATING** 5.1 EBC

FOR THE MASH

LIQUOR 11.5 litres (20 pints) **MASH TIME** 1 hr **TEMPERATURE** 65°C (149°F)

Grain bill	Quantity
Pilsner malt	3.86kg (8lb 8oz)
Carapils malt	270g (9½oz)
Flaked maize	450g (1lb)

FOR THE BOIL

LIQUOR 27 litres (47½ pints) **BOIL TIME** 1hr 15 mins

Hops	Quantity	IBU	When to add
Northern Brewer 8%	14g (½oz)	12.5	At start of boil
Crystal 3.5%	18g (⅔oz)	7.1	For last 1 hr of boil
Crystal 3.5%	28g (1oz)	3.9	For last 10 mins of boil

Other			
Protofloc	1 tsp		For last 15 mins of boil

TO FERMENT

FERMENTATION 12°C (54°F) **CONDITIONING** 4 weeks at 3°C (37°F)

Yeast
Whitelabs WLP940 Mexican lager

MALT EXTRACT VERSION

Steep 300g (10½oz) **Carapils malt** in 27 litres (47½ pints) of water at 65°C (149°F) for 30 mins. Remove the malt, then add 2.75kg (6lb 1oz) **dried light malt extract**, bring to a boil, and add the hops as specified in the main recipe.

This is an extremely crisp, dry, and well-balanced lager – thanks to the Sorachi Ace and Saaz hops. As the name suggests, flaked rice is added to the grain bill.

Japanese Rice Lager

ORIGINAL GRAVITY 1052 **EXPECTED FINAL GRAVITY** 1013 **TOTAL LIQUOR** 33 LITRES (58 PINTS)

 MAKES 23 LITRES (40 PINTS)

 READY TO DRINK 5 WEEKS

 ESTIMATED ABV 5.3%

 BITTERNESS RATING 25 IBU

 COLOUR RATING 7.3 EBC

FOR THE MASH

LIQUOR 13 litres (23 pints) **MASH TIME** 1 hr **TEMPERATURE** 65°C (149°F)

Grain bill	Quantity
Pilsner malt	4.7kg (10lb 6oz)
Flaked rice	500g (1lb 2oz)

FOR THE BOIL

LIQUOR 27 litres (47½ pints) **BOIL TIME** 1 hr 15 mins

Hops	Quantity	IBU	When to add
Sorachi Ace 14.9%	13g (½oz)	21.0	At start of boil
Sorachi Ace 14.9%	5g (¼oz)	4.0	For last 15 mins of boil
Saaz 4.2%	5g (¼oz)	0.0	At turn off

Other			
Protofloc	1 tsp		For last 15 mins of boil

TO FERMENT

FERMENTATION 12°C (54°F)
CONDITIONING 4 weeks at 3°C (37°F)

Yeast
Wyeast 2278 Czech Pils

This refreshing, light coloured Pilsner has a distinctive flavour and aroma – both spicy and floral – which is imparted by the Czech Saaz hops.

Czech Pilsner

ORIGINAL GRAVITY 1048 **EXPECTED FINAL GRAVITY** 1014 **TOTAL LIQUOR** 31.6 LITRES (55½ PINTS)

 MAKES
23 LITRES
(40 PINTS)

 READY TO DRINK
5 WEEKS

 ESTIMATED ABV
4.4%

 BITTERNESS RATING
25 IBU

 COLOUR RATING
5 EBC

FOR THE MASH

LIQUOR 11.6 litres (20½ pints) **MASH TIME** 1 hr **TEMPERATURE** 65°C (149°F)

Grain bill	Quantity
Pilsner malt	4.66kg (10lb 4oz)

FOR THE BOIL

LIQUOR 27 litres (47½ pints) **BOIL TIME** 1 hr 15 mins

Hops	Quantity	IBU	When to add
Czech Saaz 4.2%	46g (1½oz)	21.9	At start of boil
Czech Saaz 4.2%	19g (⅔oz)	3.1	For last 10 mins of boil
Czech Saaz 4.2%	19g (⅔oz)	0.0	At turn off
Other			
Protofloc	1 tsp		For last 15 mins of boil

TO FERMENT

FERMENTATION 12°C (54°F) **CONDITIONING** 4 weeks at 3°C (37°F)

Yeast
Wyeast 2001 Urquell lager

MALT EXTRACT VERSION

Add 3kg (6lb 10oz) **dried extra light malt extract** to 27 litres (47½ pints) of water, bring to a boil, and add the hops as specified in the main recipe.

The strong alcohol flavours in this Pilsner are perfectly balanced by the bitterness of the hops and by the biscuit and Carapils malts.

Imperial Pilsner

ORIGINAL GRAVITY 1079 **EXPECTED FINAL GRAVITY** 1022 **TOTAL LIQUOR** 38 LITRES (67 PINTS)

 MAKES 23 LITRES (40 PINTS)   **READY TO DRINK** 7 WEEKS   **ESTIMATED ABV** 7.7%   **BITTERNESS RATING** 60 IBU   **COLOUR RATING** 10.2 EBC

FOR THE MASH

LIQUOR 19 litres (33 pints) **MASH TIME** 1 hr **TEMPERATURE** 65°C (149°F)

Grain bill	Quantity
Pilsner malt	7.25kg (16lb)
Carapils malt	290g (10oz)
Biscuit malt	200g (7oz)

FOR THE BOIL

LIQUOR 27 litres (47½ pints) **BOIL TIME** 1 hr 15 mins

Hops	Quantity	IBU	When to add
Hallertauer Mittelfrüh 5%	110g (4oz)	25.4	At start of boil
Hallertauer Mittelfrüh 5%	73g (2½oz)	5.9	For last 10 mins of boil
Hallertauer Mittelfrüh 5%	110g (4oz)	0.0	At turn off
Other			
Protofloc	1 tsp		For last 15 mins of boil

TO FERMENT

FERMENTATION 12°C (54°F) **CONDITIONING** 6 weeks at 3°C (37°F)

Yeast
Wyeast 2124 Bohemian lager

BREWER'S TIP

Increase the amount of biscuit malt in the boil – up to 500g (1lb 2oz) – for a more toasted flavour and aroma.

MALT EXTRACT VERSION

Steep 290g (10oz) **Carapils malt** and 200g (7oz) **biscuit malt** in 27 litres (47½ pints) of water at 65°C (149°F) for 30 mins. Remove the malt, then add 4.6kg (10lb 2oz) **dried extra light malt extract**, bring to a boil, and add the hops as specified in the main recipe.

A clean, crisp beer with a fairly bitter hoppiness. These flavour characteristics were traditionally accentuated by the high sulphate content in the German water profile.

German Pilsner

ORIGINAL GRAVITY 1046 **EXPECTED FINAL GRAVITY** 1012 **TOTAL LIQUOR** 31.5 LITRES (55½ PINTS)

 MAKES
23 LITRES
(40 PINTS)

 READY TO DRINK
5 WEEKS

 ESTIMATED ABV
4.5%

 BITTERNESS RATING
30.2 IBU

 COLOUR RATING
5 EBC

FOR THE MASH

LIQUOR 11.3 litres (20 pints) **MASH TIME** 1 hr **TEMPERATURE** 65°C (149°F)

Grain bill	Quantity
Pilsner malt	4.55kg (10lb)

FOR THE BOIL

LIQUOR 27 litres (47½ pints) **BOIL TIME** 1 hr 15 mins

Hops	Quantity	IBU	When to add
Spalt Select 4.5%	50g (1¾oz)	25.7	At start of boil
Spalt Select 4.5%	25g (1oz)	4.5	For last 10 mins of boil
Spalt Select 4.5%	17g (⅔oz)	0.0	At turn off
Other			
Protofloc	1 tsp		For last 15 mins of boil

TO FERMENT

FERMENTATION 12°C (54°F) **CONDITIONING** 4 weeks at 3°C (37°F)

Yeast
Wyeast 2007 Pilsen lager

MALT EXTRACT VERSION

Add 2.9kg (6lb 6oz) **dried extra light malt extract** to 27 litres (47½ pints) of water, bring to a boil, and add the hops as specified in the main recipe.

With a rich, malty flavour and a lovely spicy, floral aroma from the Saaz hops, this easy drinking beer is devilishly moreish.

Bohemian Pilsner

ORIGINAL GRAVITY 1051 **EXPECTED FINAL GRAVITY** 1014 **TOTAL LIQUOR** 32 LITRES (56 PINTS)

 MAKES 23 LITRES (40 PINTS)   **READY TO DRINK** 4–5 WEEKS   **ESTIMATED ABV** 4.9%   **BITTERNESS RATING** 35.4 IBU   **COLOUR RATING** 6.9 EBC

FOR THE MASH

LIQUOR 12.5 litres (22 pints) **MASH TIME** 1 hr **TEMPERATURE** 65°C (149°F)

Grain bill	Quantity
Bohemian Pilsner malt	5kg (11lb)

FOR THE BOIL

LIQUOR 27 litres (47½ pints) **BOIL TIME** 1 hr 15 mins

Hops	Quantity	IBU	When to add
Saaz 4.2%	77g (2¾oz)	35.4	At start of boil
Saaz 4.2%	38g (1¼oz)	0.0	At turn off
Other			
Protofloc	1 tsp		For last 15 mins of boil

TO FERMENT

FERMENTATION 12°C (54°F) **CONDITIONING** 4 weeks at 3°C (37°F)

Yeast
Wyeast 2124 Bohemian lager

BREWER'S TIP

For a rich malt character, use a decoction mash (see p59), which involves removing part of the mash and boiling it separately to caramelize the sugars.

The corn-like maltiness of this golden beer is complemented by a hoppy aroma – a result of the late addition of American hops during the boil.

American Pilsner

ORIGINAL GRAVITY 1048 **EXPECTED FINAL GRAVITY** 1012 **TOTAL LIQUOR** 32 LITRES (56 PINTS)

MAKES
23 LITRES
(40 PINTS)

READY TO DRINK
5 WEEKS

ESTIMATED ABV
4.8%

BITTERNESS RATING
30.6 IBU

COLOUR RATING
6.4 EBC

FOR THE MASH

LIQUOR 12 litres (21 pints) **MASH TIME** 1 hr **TEMPERATURE** 65°C (149°F)

Grain bill	Quantity
Lager malt	3.5kg (7lb 11oz)
Flaked maize	1.3kg (2lb 14oz)

FOR THE BOIL

LIQUOR 27 litres (47½ pints) **BOIL TIME** 1 hr 15 mins

Hops	Quantity	IBU	When to add
Cluster 7.5%	20g (⅔oz)	16.9	At start of boil
Liberty 4.5%	15g (½oz)	2.7	For last 10 mins of boil
Crystal 3.5%	15g (½oz)	2.1	For last 10 mins of boil
Liberty 4.5%	10g (⅓oz)	1.0	For last 5 mins of boil
Crystal 3.5%	10g (⅓oz)	0.8	For last 5 mins of boil
Liberty 4.5%	32g (1oz)	0.0	At turn off
Crystal 3.5%	32g (1oz)	0.0	At turn off
Other			
Protofloc	1 tsp		For last 15 mins of boil

TO FERMENT

FERMENTATION 12°C (54°F) **CONDITIONING** 4 weeks at 3°C (37°F)

Yeast
Wyeast 2035 American lager

This beer has a lightly toasted maltiness and a clean, lager character. The Vienna malt, which is heated to a high temperature during malting, imparts a distinctive flavour.

Vienna Lager

ORIGINAL GRAVITY 1050 **EXPECTED FINAL GRAVITY** 1011 **TOTAL LIQUOR** 32 LITRES (56 PINTS)

 MAKES 23 LITRES (40 PINTS)

 READY TO DRINK 5 WEEKS

 ESTIMATED ABV 5.1%

 BITTERNESS RATING 26.5 IBU

 COLOUR RATING 19.7 EBC

FOR THE MASH

LIQUOR 12 litres (21 pints) **MASH TIME** 1 hr **TEMPERATURE** 65°C (149°F)

Grain bill	Quantity
Vienna malt	4.16kg (9lb 3oz)
Munich malt	670g (1lb 7oz)
Melanoidin malt	125g (4½oz)
Chocolate malt	50g (1¾oz)

FOR THE BOIL

LIQUOR 27 litres (47½ pints) **BOIL TIME** 1 hr 15 mins

Hops	Quantity	IBU	When to add
Northern Brewer 8%	30g (1oz)	20.1	At start of boil
Hallertauer Hersbrucker 3.5%	15g (½oz)	0.0	At turn off
Tettnang 4.5%	15g (½oz)	0.0	At turn off
Other			
Protofloc	1 tsp		For last 15 mins of boil

TO FERMENT

FERMENTATION 12°C (54°F) **CONDITIONING** 4 weeks at 3°C (37°F)

Yeast
Whitelabs WLP830 German

BREWER'S TIP

For a slightly citrus finish, try using the same quantity of Liberty hops at the end of the boil instead of the Tettnang.

This German beer is traditionally brewed in spring, lagered in cold cellars or caves over the summer, and then served at the Oktoberfest celebrations in autumn.

Oktoberfest

ORIGINAL GRAVITY 1057 **EXPECTED FINAL GRAVITY** 1017 **TOTAL LIQUOR** 32 LITRES (56 PINTS)

 MAKES 23 LITRES (40 PINTS)

 **READY TO DRINK** 5 WEEKS

 ESTIMATED ABV 5.3%

 BITTERNESS RATING 25.2 IBU

COLOUR RATING 13.6 EBC

FOR THE MASH

LIQUOR 12 litres (21 pints) **MASH TIME** 1 hr **TEMPERATURE** 65°C (149°F)

Grain bill	Quantity
Vienna malt	4kg (8lb 13oz)
Munich malt	800g (1lb 12oz)
Carapils	750g (1lb 10oz)
Crystal malt	100g (3½oz)

FOR THE BOIL

LIQUOR 27 litres (47½ pints) **BOIL TIME** 1 hr 15 mins

Hops	Quantity	IBU	When to add
Perle 8%	27g (1oz)	23.1	At start of boil
Hallertauer Mittelfrüh 5%	5g (¼oz)	2.1	For last 30 mins of boil

Other			
Protofloc	1 tsp		For last 15 mins of boil

TO FERMENT

FERMENTATION 12°C (54°F) **CONDITIONING** 4 weeks at 3°C (37°F)

Yeast
Whitelabs WLP820 Oktoberfest

BREWER'S TIP

This beer will benefit from extended ageing at cellar temperatures for as many weeks as you can handle before giving in to temptation!

A recent addition to the Bock family of beers, this brew uses the Hella Bock yeast, which delivers a clean finish and leaves a taste of both malt and hops in the mouth.

Helles Bock

ORIGINAL GRAVITY 1072 **EXPECTED FINAL GRAVITY** 1019 **TOTAL LIQUOR** 35 LITRES (61½ PINTS)

 MAKES 23 LITRES (40 PINTS)

 READY TO DRINK 7 WEEKS

 ESTIMATED ABV 7.1%

 BITTERNESS RATING 32 IBU

 COLOUR RATING 17.5 EBC

FOR THE MASH

LIQUOR 18 litres (31½ pints) **MASH TIME** 1 hr **TEMPERATURE** 65°C (149°F)

Grain bill	Quantity
Pilsner malt	3.75kg (8lb 4oz)
Munich malt	2.47kg (5lb 7oz)
Belgian aromatic malt	600g (1lb 5oz)
Melanoidin malt	250g (9oz)

FOR THE BOIL

LIQUOR 27 litres (47½ pints) **BOIL TIME** 1 hr 15 mins

Hops	Quantity	IBU	When to add
Northern Brewer 8%	40g (1⅓oz)	30.2	At start of boil
Spalt Select 4.5%	10g (⅓oz)	2.0	For last 15 mins of boil
Spalt Select 4.5%	8g (¼oz)	0.0	At turn off
Other			
Protofloc	1tsp		For last 15 mins of boil

TO FERMENT

FERMENTATION 12°C (54°F) **CONDITIONING** 6 weeks at 3°C (37°F)

Yeast
Wyeast 2487 Hella Bock

BREWER'S TIP

If the Hella Bock yeast is not available, try using Wyeast 2124 Bohemian lager instead.

First brewed in Einbeck, Germany, in the 1300s, and later adapted by brewers in Munich, Bock is a dark, strong, malty lager with a very low hop flavour and aroma.

Traditional Bock

ORIGINAL GRAVITY 1064 **EXPECTED FINAL GRAVITY** 1015 **TOTAL LIQUOR** 35 LITRES (61½ PINTS)

 MAKES 23 LITRES (40 PINTS)

 READY TO DRINK 5 WEEKS

 ESTIMATED ABV 6.5%

 BITTERNESS RATING 22 IBU

 COLOUR RATING 29.1 EBC

FOR THE MASH

LIQUOR 19 litres (33 pints) **MASH TIME** 1 hr **TEMPERATURE** 65°C (149°F)

Grain bill	Quantity
Pale malt	2.75kg (6lb 1oz)
Munich malt	2.75kg (6lb 1oz)
Carapils malt	550g (1lb 3oz)
Special B malt	350g (12oz)

FOR THE BOIL

LIQUOR 27 litres (47½ pints) **BOIL TIME** 1 hr 15 mins

Hops	Quantity	IBU	When to add
Northern Brewer 8%	24g (¾oz)	18.9	At start of boil
Tettnang 4.5%	10g (⅓oz)	3.2	For last 30 mins of boil
Other			
Protofloc	1 tsp		For last 15 mins of boil

TO FERMENT

FERMENTATION 12°C (54°F) **CONDITIONING** 4 weeks at 3°C (37°F)

Yeast
Wyeast 2206 Bohemian lager

Stronger and maltier than Traditional Bock (see p100), this beer was first brewed by monks more than 200 years ago and served as "liquid bread" during times of fasting.

Doppelbock

ORIGINAL GRAVITY 1075 **EXPECTED FINAL GRAVITY** 1021 **TOTAL LIQUOR** 35 LITRES (61½ PINTS)

MAKES 23 LITRES (40 PINTS) **READY TO DRINK** 7 WEEKS **ESTIMATED ABV** 7.3% **BITTERNESS RATING** 20.7 IBU **COLOUR RATING** 31.8 EBC

FOR THE MASH

LIQUOR 18.9 litres (33 pints) **MASH TIME** 1 hr **TEMPERATURE** 65°C (149°F)

Grain bill	Quantity
Pilsner malt	2.8kg (6lb 3oz)
Munich malt	4.2kg (9lb 4oz)
Caramunich II	286g (10oz)
Carafa special II malt	114g (4oz)

FOR THE BOIL

LIQUOR 27 litres (47½ pints) **BOIL TIME** 1 hr 10 mins

Hops	Quantity	IBU	When to add
Perle 8%	20g (⅔oz)	14.4	At start of boil
Tettnang 4.5%	20g (⅔oz)	6.0	For last 30 mins of boil
Other			
Protofloc	1 tsp		For last 15 mins of boil

TO FERMENT

FERMENTATION 12°C (54°F) **CONDITIONING** 6 weeks at 3°C (37°F)

Yeast
Wyeast 2124 Bohemian lager

DOPPELBOCK

Eisbock is a rich, intense brew with a malty flavour and a deep colour. It is high in alcohol and has a slight, lingering chocolate flavour on the finish – a beer to be savoured.

Eisbock

ORIGINAL GRAVITY 1113 **EXPECTED FINAL GRAVITY** 1026 **TOTAL LIQUOR** 40 LITRES (70 PINTS)

 MAKES 23 LITRES (40 PINTS)

 READY TO DRINK 7 WEEKS

 ESTIMATED ABV 11.8%

 BITTERNESS RATING 30.4 IBU

 COLOUR RATING 40 EBC

FOR THE MASH

LIQUOR 27 litres (47½ pints) **MASH TIME** 1 hr **TEMPERATURE** 65°C (149°F)

Grain bill	Quantity
Pale malt	4.75kg (10lb 7oz)
Munich malt	5.7kg (12½lb)
Flaked barley	380g (13½oz)
Chocolate malt	100g (3½oz)
Carafa special I malt	95g (3⅓oz)

FOR THE BOIL

LIQUOR 27 litres (47½ pints) **BOIL TIME** 1 hr 15 mins

Hops	Quantity	IBU	When to add
Northern Brewer 8%	32g (1oz)	17.4	At start of boil
Perle 8%	32g (1oz)	13.0	For last 30 mins of boil

Other			
Protofloc	1 tsp		For last 15 mins of boil

TO FERMENT

FERMENTATION 12°C (54°F) **CONDITIONING** 6 weeks at 3°C (37°F)

Yeast
Wyeast 2308 Munich lager

This delicious dark lager is lightly hopped with floral Hersbrucker and Perle hops. The end result is a smooth beer with a crisp finish.

Dark American Lager

ORIGINAL GRAVITY 1055 **EXPECTED FINAL GRAVITY** 1013 **TOTAL LIQUOR** 33 LITRES (58 PINTS)

 MAKES 23 LITRES (40 PINTS) **READY TO DRINK** 5 WEEKS **ESTIMATED ABV** 5.6% **BITTERNESS RATING** 19 IBU **COLOUR RATING** 31.9 EBC

FOR THE MASH

LIQUOR 14 litres (24½ pints) **MASH TIME** 1 hr **TEMPERATURE** 65°C (149°F)

Grain bill	Quantity
Pilsner malt	3.54kg (7lb 13oz)
Munich malt	766g (1lb 11oz)
Flaked maize	709g (1lb 9oz)
Special B	300g (10½oz)
Crystal malt 60L	153g (5⅓oz)
Carafa special III malt	50g (1¾oz)

FOR THE BOIL

LIQUOR 27 litres (47½ pints) **BOIL TIME** 1 hr 15 mins

Hops	Quantity	IBU	When to add
Northern Brewer 8%	22g (¾oz)	18.9	At start of boil
Perle 8%	6g (¼oz)	0.2	For last 1 min of boil
Hallertauer Hersbrucker 3.5%	10g (⅓oz)	0.0	At turn off
Other			
Protofloc	1 tsp		For last 15 mins of boil

TO FERMENT

FERMENTATION 12°C (54°F) **CONDITIONING** 4 weeks at 3°C (37°F)

Yeast
Wyeast 2035 American lager

Hints of chocolate and caramel marry perfectly with the rich, malty sweetness of the Munich malt here. The result is a lager full of character with a classic, smooth finish.

Munich Dunkel

ORIGINAL GRAVITY 1055 **EXPECTED FINAL GRAVITY** 1013 **TOTAL LIQUOR** 33 LITRES (58 PINTS)

 MAKES 23 LITRES (40 PINTS)

 READY TO DRINK 5 WEEKS

 ESTIMATED ABV 5.5%

 BITTERNESS RATING 27.4 IBU

 COLOUR RATING 34.4 EBC

FOR THE MASH

LIQUOR 14 litres (24½ pints) **MASH TIME** 1 hr **TEMPERATURE** 65°C (149°F)

Grain bill	Quantity
Lager malt	2kg (4½lb)
Munich malt	3kg (6lb 10oz)
Biscuit malt	200g (7oz)
Chocolate wheat	100g (3½oz)
Carafa special II malt	80g (2¾oz)

FOR THE BOIL

LIQUOR 27 litres (47½ pints) **BOIL TIME** 1 hr 15 mins

Hops	Quantity	IBU	When to add
Magnum 11%	23g (¾oz)	26.9	At start of boil
Hallertauer Mittelfrüh 5%	5g (¼oz)	0.5	For last 5 mins of boil
Hallertauer Mittelfrüh 5%	9g (⅓oz)	0.0	At turn off
Other			
Protofloc	1 tsp		For last 15 mins of boil

TO FERMENT

FERMENTATION 12°C (54°F) **CONDITIONING** 4 weeks at 3°C (37°F)

Yeast
Fermentis W34/70

BREWER'S TIP

A triple-decoction mash (see p59) will give an enhanced maltiness to the beer and a greater depth of colour.

As black as a stout but with a clean, refreshing, and light lager finish, this is a fantastic and unusual beer that will surprise and impress.

Black Lager

ORIGINAL GRAVITY 1051 **EXPECTED FINAL GRAVITY** 1012 **TOTAL LIQUOR** 32 LITRES (56 PINTS)

 MAKES
23 LITRES (40 PINTS)

 READY TO DRINK
5 WEEKS

 ESTIMATED ABV
5.1%

 BITTERNESS RATING
38 IBU

 COLOUR RATING
57 EBC

FOR THE MASH

LIQUOR 13 litres (23 pints) **MASH TIME** 1 hr **TEMPERATURE** 65°C (149°F)

Grain bill	Quantity
Pale malt	4.5kg (10lb)
Melanoidin malt	250g (9oz)
Chocolate malt	100g (3½oz)
Carafa special III malt	150g (5½oz)

FOR THE BOIL

LIQUOR 27 litres (47½ pints) **BOIL TIME** 1 hr 15 mins

Hops	Quantity	IBU	When to add
Centennial 8.5%	32g (1oz)	28.5	At start of boil
Hallertauer Hersbrucker 3.5%	54g (2oz)	9.9	For last 15 mins of boil
Hallertauer Hersbrucker 3.5%	46g (1½oz)	0.0	At turn off
Other			
Protofloc	1 tsp		For last 15 mins of boil

TO FERMENT

FERMENTATION 14°C (57°F) **CONDITIONING** 4 weeks at 3°C (37°F)

Yeast
Wyeast 2042 Danish lager

MALT EXTRACT VERSION

Steep 250g (9oz) **melanoidin malt**, 100g (3½oz) **chocolate malt**, and 150g (5½oz) **Carafa special III malt** in 27 litres (47½ pints) of water at 65°C (149°F) for 30 mins. Remove, then add 3.3kg (7lb 4oz) **dried extra light malt extract**, bring to a boil, and add hops as specified in the main recipe.

Ales

A popular choice among home brewers, ale is quick and easy to produce as it can be brewed at room temperature and has a short conditioning period.

Ale is a full-flavoured style of beer with a long history. In the Middle Ages, for example, it was a source of hydration and nutrition, with low-alcohol ales (known as "small beers") being consumed throughout the day due to the lack of availability of safe, fresh water.

TOP-FERMENTING YEAST
Modern ales are brewed at 16–22°C (61–72°F) using top-fermenting yeasts – yeasts that rise to the surface of the wort during primary fermentation. These conditions allow the yeast to create lots of flavour compounds and esters, which can impart a wide range of complex fruit and malt flavours to the finished brew.

MALTS AND HOPS
Most of the fermentable sugars in ale wort come from pale, malted barley, which is blended with darker malts for extra character. Hops are also used in all ales – in varying quantities. They provide bitterness, flavour and aroma, help preserve the beer, and balance the taste of the alcohol. With a huge number of malt types and hop varieties available (see pp22–31) the possibilities for the adventurous home-brewer are seemingly endless.

Ales are generally served cool, but not cold, to allow the malt and hop flavours and aromas to fully develop. Carbonation levels are typically low and, for authenticity, ales are best stored in – and served from – a barrel or keg, rather than bottles.

Pale ale

Traditionally brewed with a large proportion of pale malts, and with soft water, pale ale has a smooth, balanced bitterness.

- **Appearance** Pale straw to light golden with a small, lingering head.

- **Taste** Smooth and creamy with subtle hop bitterness. Flavours from the yeast influence its character.

- **Aroma** A light maltiness, with a hop aroma determined by the variety – English hops, for example, will impart subtle floral notes.

- **Strength** 4–6% ABV

- **GB** English pale ales have a light floral character and are not too bitter. There may be a slight butterscotch finish.

- **BE** Belgian pale ales are strong, with spicy flavours from the Belgian yeast.

- **US** American pale ales have a very hoppy, citrus character and a clean, dry finish.

See pp112–30

India pale ale (IPA)

Created to withstand long sea journeys, IPA has high hop and alcohol levels.

- **Appearance** Light straw to deep golden in colour; good clarity with a thin, lingering head.

- **Taste** Strong, spicy alcohol flavours with smooth bitterness and a dry finish.

- **Aroma** Moderately hoppy; malt and caramel aromas are also common.

- **Strength** 5–7.5% ABV

- (GB) English IPAs have subtle floral and spicy hop aromas. Although they can have an assertive bitterness, this is usually well balanced by the alcohol content.

- (US) American IPAs have intense citrus hop aromas and flavours from the use of American hops. They are stronger than British IPAs, with an increased bitterness.

 See pp131–36

Sour and lambic ales

The wild yeast used in these ales produces a sourness, often balanced by fruity or spicy notes.

- **Appearance** Varies by style, but often fruit-coloured. Usually fairly hazy with a creamy head.

- **Taste** Depends on the style, but generally sweet, sour, sharp, and very distinct.

- **Aroma** High fruit aromas, often with spicy notes.

- **Strength** 3.2–7% ABV

- (BE) Belgian varieties are typically high in alcohol, with the extended ageing period creating a complex, flavourful beer akin to a fine red wine.

- (DE) German varieties are sour, mildly fruity, highly carbonated, and have a very dry finish. They are low in alcohol and have a creamy, long-lasting head.

See pp137–39

Bitter

Often a commercial brewer's main beer, bitter has low carbonation levels and is best served from a cask via a hand pump.

- **Appearance** Light gold to deep copper, with good clarity and a light head.

- **Taste** More bitter than sweet, but still perfectly balanced. Caramel or light fruit flavours are common.

- **Aroma** Moderate to light hop aromas, with malt and sometimes caramel notes.

- **Strength** 3.2–6% ABV

- (GB) English bitters are lightly hopped, fairly low in strength, and have a sweetish finish with hints of fruit. Scottish bitters, which are fermented at lower temperatures, are cleaner and drier-tasting.

See pp140–49

Strong ale

Often brewed for special occasions, strong ale is best enjoyed in moderation. Most will benefit from extended conditioning and ageing.

- **Appearance** Light copper to deep red, with a lasting off-white head. Sometimes slightly hazy.
- **Taste** Varies by style, but usually spicy and malty, often with fruit flavours from the fermentation process.
- **Aroma** Little or no hop aroma, with malt and caramel characters.
- **Strength** 6–9% ABV
- (GB) English strong ales are often spiced with festive herbs and spices to create a delicious, complex beer. They are strong and deep amber in colour.
- (BE) Belgian strong ales, which are brewed all year round, are pale in colour and have distinct spicy flavours and aromas from the unique yeast strains.

See pp150–59

Brown ale

A traditional English style that is becoming rare. Brown ale is mainly brewed in the north of England as demand has fallen elsewhere.

- **Appearance** Dark amber to reddish brown, with an off-white head.
- **Taste** Nutty with caramel and biscuit notes; a medium bitterness balances the sweetness.
- **Aroma** Light hop aroma, with noticeable malts and caramel.
- **Strength** 2.8–5.4% ABV
- (GB) Northern English brown ales are strong, malty, and nutty, while those from the south are usually darker, sweeter, and lower in alcohol.

See pp160–63

Mild

A low-gravity, light-flavoured beer created for drinking in quantity. Although becoming rare, mild is still popular in parts of England.

- **Appearance** Deep copper to dark brown, with a light, short-lived head.
- **Taste** Light with subtle hop flavours; surprisingly flavourful for the low alcohol content.
- **Aroma** Little or no hop aroma, with caramel, biscuit, and roasted characters.
- **Strength** 2.8–4.5% ABV
- (GB) Traditionally, mild was popular in the English Midlands, where the refreshing and inexpensive brew was consumed by industrial workers.

 See pp164–65

Barley wine

So-called because it has the high strength and complex flavours often associated with wine, barley wine is particularly alchoholic.

- **Appearance** Deep golden to dark amber. Due to the high alcohol content, it will leave legs, or streaks, on the glass when swirled.

- **Taste** Sweet and complex malt flavours, including caramel, dried fruit, nut, and toffee-like notes.

- **Aroma** Some hop aroma, with strong malt and caramel characters. Vintage versions are almost sherry-like.

- **Strength** 8–12% ABV

- (GB) English barley wines are intense with complex fruit and caramel flavours. A subtle bitterness and hop flavour balances the high alcohol content.

- (US) American barley wines have increased hop bitterness balanced with complex malt flavours, and often citrusy notes.

 See pp166–68

Porter

Originating in 18th-century London and descended from brown ale, porter was drunk by street and river porters – hence the name.

- **Appearance** Dark brown or black.

- **Taste** Mild roast flavours, a rich maltiness, and sometimes with hints of liquorice.

- **Aroma** Roasted notes, with a slight chocolate character, maltiness, and a subtle smokiness.

- **Strength** 4–7% ABV

- (EU) Baltic porter – originally brewed in the Baltic states – is typically high in alcohol, with a sweet, malty character. It is often bottom-fermented like a lager.

See pp169–73

Stout

Closely related to porter, stout was first known as "stout porter" – a stronger version of the style. It is full-bodied and very dark in colour.

- **Appearance** Very dark brown to jet-black. Often served using nitrogen to create a thick, creamy, tan head with no carbonation.

- **Taste** Roasted and burnt bitter flavours; a smooth, creamy mouthfeel; low to moderate hop bitterness.

- **Aroma** Roasted coffee aromas, sometimes with a chocolate-like character; low or no hop aroma.

- **Strength** 4–7% ABV

- (IE) Irish stout is the classic dry stout – with a famously thick and creamy head.

- (GB) London stout has a lower gravity than other versions and can be quite sweet.

- (US) American stout has a strong hop bitterness and aroma.

See pp174–81

Zingy citrus flavours and aromas from the Galaxy and Wai-ti hops help make this a particularly refreshing beer with a balanced malty finish.

Spring Beer

ORIGINAL GRAVITY 1046 **EXPECTED FINAL GRAVITY** 1012 **TOTAL LIQUOR** 31.5 LITRES (55½ PINTS)

 MAKES 23 LITRES (40 PINTS)   **READY TO DRINK** 5 WEEKS   **ESTIMATED ABV** 4.5%   **BITTERNESS RATING** 34.6 IBU **COLOUR RATING** 9.3 EBC

FOR THE MASH

LIQUOR 11.25 litres (20 pints) **MASH TIME** 1 hr **TEMPERATURE** 65°C (149°F)

Grain bill	Quantity
Pale malt	4kg (8lb 13oz)
Munich malt	500g (1lb 2oz)

FOR THE BOIL

LIQUOR 27 litres (47½ pints) **BOIL TIME** 1 hr 10 mins

Hops	Quantity	IBU	When to add
Galaxy 14.4%	30g (1oz)	34.6	At start of boil
Galaxy 14.4%	30g (1oz)	0.0	At turn off
Wai-ti 4.5%	30g (1oz)	0.0	At turn off
Other			
Protofloc	1 tsp		For last 15 mins of boil

TO FERMENT

FERMENTATION 18°C (64°F) **CONDITIONING** 4 weeks at 12°C (54°F)

Yeast
Wyeast 1275 Thames Valley ale

BREWER'S TIP

For an extra fruity aroma, try dry hopping (see p65) with 25g (scant 1oz) Wai-ti hops in the fermenter for 4 days.

Tawny coloured and with a malty flavour, the dried elderflowers added to the boil give this ale a subtle yet unmistakably fruity finish, with a hint of peach.

Elderflower Ale

ORIGINAL GRAVITY 1045 **EXPECTED FINAL GRAVITY** 1011 **TOTAL LIQUOR** 31.5 LITRES (55½ PINTS)

 MAKES
23 LITRES
(40 PINTS)

 READY TO DRINK
5 WEEKS

 ESTIMATED ABV
4.5%

 BITTERNESS RATING
36.6 IBU

 COLOUR RATING
13.5 EBC

FOR THE MASH

LIQUOR 11.2 litres (20 pints) **MASH TIME** 1 hr **TEMPERATURE** 65°C (149°F)

Grain bill	Quantity
Pale malt	4.3kg (9lb 8oz)
Crystal malt	100g (3½oz)
Chocolate malt	16g (½oz)

FOR THE BOIL

LIQUOR 27 litres (47½ pints) **BOIL TIME** 1 hr 10 mins

Hops	Quantity	IBU	When to add
Challenger 7%	56g (2oz)	31.5	At start of boil
Dried elderflowers	15g (½oz)	0.0	For last 15 mins
Fuggle 4.5%	28g (1oz)	5.1	For last 10 mins
Challenger 7%	17g (⅔oz)	0.0	At turn off

Other			
Protofloc	1 tsp		For last 15 mins of boil

TO FERMENT

FERMENTATION 20°C (68°F) **CONDITIONING** 4 weeks at 12°C (54°F)

Yeast
Wyeast 1275 Thames Valley ale

MALT EXTRACT VERSION

Steep 100g (3½oz) **crystal malt** and 16g (½oz) **chocolate malt** in 27 litres (47½ pints) of water at 65°C (149°F) for 30 mins. Remove the malt, then add 2.75kg (6lb 1oz) **dried malt extract**, bring to a boil, and add the hops and elderflowers as specified in the main recipe.

This delightful pale ale celebrates the autumn grain harvest and heralds the change of seasons. It is a fresh, crisp brew with a grainy flavour and citrus finish.

Harvest Pale Ale

ORIGINAL GRAVITY 1041 **EXPECTED FINAL GRAVITY** 1010 **TOTAL LIQUOR** 31.5 LITRES (55½ PINTS)

 MAKES 23 LITRES (40 PINTS)
 READY TO DRINK 5 WEEKS
 ESTIMATED ABV 4.2%
  BITTERNESS RATING 41 IBU
 COLOUR RATING 11 EBC

FOR THE MASH

LIQUOR 10.25 litres (18 pints) **MASH TIME** 1 hr **TEMPERATURE** 65°C (149°F)

Grain bill	Quantity
Lager malt	3.7kg (8lb 2oz)
Vienna malt	200g (7oz)
Crystal wheat malt	200g (7oz)

FOR THE BOIL

LIQUOR 27 litres (47½ pints) **BOIL TIME** 1 hr 10 mins

Hops	Quantity	IBU	When to add
Magnum 16%	21g (¾oz)	39.3	At start of boil
Willamette 6.3%	7g (¼oz)	1.8	For last 10 mins of boil
Willamette 6.3%	20g (⅔oz)	0.0	At turn off
Cascade 6.6%	20g (⅔oz)	0.0	At turn off
Other			
Protofloc	1 tsp		For last 15 mins of boil

TO FERMENT

FERMENTATION 18°C (64°F) **CONDITIONING** 4 weeks at 12°C (54°F)

Yeast
Whitelabs WLP060 American ale blend

ESB, or "Extra Special Bitter", is traditionally brewed as a premium pale ale. Strong, malty, and with a slightly fruity, caramel finish, it is dangerously drinkable!

ESB Ale

ORIGINAL GRAVITY 1054 EXPECTED FINAL GRAVITY 1016 TOTAL LIQUOR 32.5 LITRES (57 PINTS)

 **MAKES** 23 LITRES (40 PINTS)   **READY TO DRINK** 5 WEEKS   **ESTIMATED ABV** 5.1%   **BITTERNESS RATING** 32.5 IBU   **COLOUR RATING** 16.2 EBC

FOR THE MASH

LIQUOR 13.5 litres (24 pints) **MASH TIME** 1 hr **TEMPERATURE** 65°C (149°F)

Grain bill	Quantity
Pale malt	5kg (11lb)
Crystal malt	224g (8oz)
Torrified wheat	115g (4oz)
Chocolate malt	17g (⅔oz)

FOR THE BOIL

LIQUOR 27 litres (47½ pints) **BOIL TIME** 1 hr 10 mins

Hops	Quantity	IBU	When to add
Challenger 7%	38g (1¼oz)	28.4	At start of boil
East Kent Golding 5.5%	20g (⅔oz)	4.1	For last 10 mins of boil
Fuggle 4.5%	13g (½oz)	0.0	At turn off
Other			
Protofloc	1 tsp		For last 15 mins of boil

TO FERMENT

FERMENTATION 20°C (68°F) **CONDITIONING** 4 weeks at 12°C (54°F)

Yeast
Wyeast 1187 Ringwood ale

MALT EXTRACT VERSION

Steep 224g (8oz) **crystal malt** and 17g (⅔oz) **chocolate malt** in 27 litres (47½ pints) of water at 65°C (149°F) for 30 mins. Remove the malt, then add 3kg (6lb 10oz) **dried malt extract** and 250g (9oz) **dried wheat malt extract**, bring to a boil, and add the hops as specified in the main recipe.

ALES PALE ALE

Amarillo is one of the most pungent varieties of hops available, and my personal favourite. The powerful citrus aromas will fill the air as soon as you open the packet.

Amarillo Single Hop Ale

ORIGINAL GRAVITY 1050 EXPECTED FINAL GRAVITY 1012 TOTAL LIQUOR 32 LITRES (56 PINTS)

 MAKES 23 LITRES (40 PINTS)   **READY TO DRINK** 7 WEEKS   **ESTIMATED ABV** 5%   **BITTERNESS RATING** 40 IBU   **COLOUR RATING** 10 EBC

FOR THE MASH

LIQUOR 12.3 litres (21½ pints) **MASH TIME** 1 hr **TEMPERATURE** 65°C (149°F)

Grain bill	Quantity
Pale malt	4.7kg (10lb 6oz)
Carapils malt	235g (8¼oz)

FOR THE BOIL

LIQUOR 27 litres (47½ pints) **BOIL TIME** 1 hr 10 mins

Hops	Quantity	IBU	When to add
Amarillo 5%	54g (2oz)	29.9	At start of boil
Amarillo 5%	27g (1oz)	7.2	For last 15 mins of boil
Amarillo 5%	27g (1oz)	2.9	For last 5 mins of boil
Amarillo 5%	83g (3oz)	0.0	At turn off
Other			
Protofloc	1 tsp		For last 15 mins of boil

TO FERMENT

FERMENTATION 18°C (64°F) **CONDITIONING** 6 weeks at 12°C (54°F)

Yeast
Wyeast 1056 American ale

MALT EXTRACT VERSION

Steep 235g (8¼oz) **Carapils malt** in 27 litres (47½ pints) of water at 65°C (149°F) for 30 mins. Remove the malt, then add 3kg (6lb 10oz) **dried light malt extract**, bring to a boil, and add the hops as specified in the main recipe.

The delicious gooseberry aromas of this unique hop are reminiscent of the Sauvignon Blanc grape variety, which is how the hop gets its name.

Nelson Sauvin Single Hop Ale

ORIGINAL GRAVITY 1050 **EXPECTED FINAL GRAVITY** 1012 **TOTAL LIQUOR** 32 LITRES (56 PINTS)

 MAKES 23 LITRES (40 PINTS)

 READY TO DRINK 7 WEEKS

 ESTIMATED ABV 5%

 BITTERNESS RATING 40 IBU

 COLOUR RATING 10 EBC

FOR THE MASH

LIQUOR 12.3 litres (21½ pints) **MASH TIME** 1 hr **TEMPERATURE** 65°C (149°F)

Grain bill	Quantity
Pale malt	4.7kg (10lb 6oz)
Carapils malt	235g (8¼oz)

FOR THE BOIL

LIQUOR 27 litres (47½ pints) **BOIL TIME** 1 hr 10 mins

Hops	Quantity	IBU	When to add
Nelson Sauvin 12.5%	22g (¾oz)	29.9	At start of boil
Nelson Sauvin 12.5%	11g (⅓oz)	7.2	For last 15 mins of boil
Nelson Sauvin 12.5%	11g (⅓oz)	2.9	For last 5 mins of boil
Nelson Sauvin 12.5%	33g (1¼oz)	0.0	At turn off
Other			
Protofloc	1 tsp		For last 15 mins of boil

TO FERMENT

FERMENTATION 18°C (64°F) **CONDITIONING** 6 weeks at 12°C (54°F)

Yeast
Wyeast 1056 American ale

MALT EXTRACT VERSION

Steep 235g (8¼oz) **Carapils malt** in 27 litres (47½ pints) of water at 65°C (149°F) for 30 mins. Remove the malt, then add 3kg (6lb 10oz) **dried light malt extract**, bring to a boil, and add the hops as specified in the main recipe.

East Kent Golding is a classic English hop and a favourite among brewers. With a subtle aroma that is both floral and slightly spicy, it creates a finely balanced beer.

East Kent Golding Single Hop Ale

ORIGINAL GRAVITY 1050 **EXPECTED FINAL GRAVITY** 1012 **TOTAL LIQUOR** 32 LITRES (56 PINTS)

 MAKES 23 LITRES (40 PINTS)

 READY TO DRINK 7 WEEKS

 ESTIMATED ABV 5%

 BITTERNESS RATING 40 IBU

 COLOUR RATING 10 EBC

FOR THE MASH

LIQUOR 12.3 litres (21½ pints) **MASH TIME** 1 hr **TEMPERATURE** 65°C (149°F)

Grain bill	Quantity
Pale malt	4.7kg (10lb 6oz)
Carapils malt	235g (8¼oz)

FOR THE BOIL

LIQUOR 27 litres (47½ pints) **BOIL TIME** 1 hr 10 mins

Hops	Quantity	IBU	When to add
East Kent Golding 5.5%	49g (1¾oz)	29.9	At start of boil
East Kent Golding 5.5%	24g (¾oz)	7.2	For last 15 mins of boil
East Kent Golding 5.5%	24g (¾oz)	2.9	For last 5 mins of boil
East Kent Golding 5.5%	75g (2½oz)	0.0	At turn off

Other			
Protofloc	1 tsp		For last 15 mins of boil

TO FERMENT

FERMENTATION 18°C (64°F) **CONDITIONING** 6 weeks at 12°C (54°F)

Yeast
Wyeast 1056 American ale

MALT EXTRACT VERSION

Steep 235g (8¼oz) **Carapils malt** in 27 litres (47½ pints) of water at 65°C (149°F) for 30 mins. Remove the malt, then add 3kg (6lb 10oz) **dried light malt extract**, bring to a boil, and add the hops as specified in the main recipe.

BREWER'S TIP

For an extra hoppy aroma, try dry hopping (see p65) with 30g (1oz) East Kent Golding hops in the fermenter for 4 days.

A classic "noble" hop – one of four varieties originating in central Europe and prized for their aroma – Saaz imparts a floral aroma and spicy character to this ale.

Saaz Single Hop Ale

ORIGINAL GRAVITY 1050 **EXPECTED FINAL GRAVITY** 1012 **TOTAL LIQUOR** 32 LITRES (56 PINTS)

 MAKES
23 LITRES
(40 PINTS)

 READY TO DRINK
7 WEEKS

 ESTIMATED ABV
5%

 BITTERNESS RATING
40 IBU

COLOUR RATING
10 EBC

FOR THE MASH

LIQUOR 12.3 litres (21½ pints) **MASH TIME** 1 hr **TEMPERATURE** 65°C (149°F)

Grain bill	Quantity
Pale malt	4.7kg (10lb 6oz)
Carapils malt	235g (8¼oz)

FOR THE BOIL

LIQUOR 27 litres (47½ pints) **BOIL TIME** 1 hr 10 mins

Hops	Quantity	IBU	When to add
Saaz 4.2%	64g (2¼oz)	29.9	At start of boil
Saaz 4.2%	32g (1oz)	7.2	For last 15 mins of boil
Saaz 4.2%	32g (1oz)	2.9	For last 5 mins of boil
Saaz 4.2%	99g (3½oz)	0.0	At turn off
Other			
Protofloc	1 tsp		For last 15 mins of boil

TO FERMENT

FERMENTATION 18°C (64°F) **CONDITIONING** 6 weeks at 12°C (54°F)

Yeast
Wyeast 1056 American ale

MALT EXTRACT VERSION

Steep 235g (8¼oz) **Carapils malt** in 27 litres (47½ pints) of water at 65°C (149°F) for 30 mins. Remove the malt, then add 3kg (6lb 10oz) **dried light malt extract**, bring to a boil, and add the hops as specified in the main recipe.

The floral and citrus qualities of Cascade make it a popular choice of hops among brewers. It is subtler than other citrus varieties, and has notes of grapefruit.

Cascade Single Hop Ale

ORIGINAL GRAVITY 1050 EXPECTED FINAL GRAVITY 1012 TOTAL LIQUOR 32 LITRES (56 PINTS)

 MAKES 23 LITRES (40 PINTS)   **READY TO DRINK** 7 WEEKS   **ESTIMATED ABV** 5%   **BITTERNESS RATING** 40 IBU   **COLOUR RATING** 10 EBC

FOR THE MASH

LIQUOR 12.3 litres (21½ pints) **MASH TIME** 1 hr **TEMPERATURE** 65°C (149°F)

Grain bill	Quantity
Pale malt	4.7kg (10lb 6oz)
Carapils malt	235g (8¼oz)

FOR THE BOIL

LIQUOR 27 litres (47½ pints) **BOIL TIME** 1 hr 10 mins

Hops	Quantity	IBU	When to add
Cascade 6.6%	41g (1½oz)	29.9	At start of boil
Cascade 6.6%	20g (⅔oz)	7.2	For last 15 mins of boil
Cascade 6.6%	20g (⅔oz)	2.9	For last 5 mins of boil
Cascade 6.6%	63g (2¼oz)	0.0	At turn off

Other			
Protofloc	1 tsp		For last 15 mins of boil

TO FERMENT

FERMENTATION 18°C (64°F) **CONDITIONING** 6 weeks at 12°C (54°F)

Yeast
Wyeast 1056 American ale

MALT EXTRACT VERSION

Steep 235g (8¼oz) **Carapils malt** in 27 litres (47½ pints) of water at 65°C (149°F) for 30 mins. Remove the malt, then add 3kg (6lb 10oz) **dried light malt extract**, bring to a boil, and add the hops as specified in the main recipe.

A golden-coloured ale with a delicious floral aroma, the low gravity of the wort – and low alcohol level of the final brew – makes this a great session beer.

Pale Ale

ORIGINAL GRAVITY 1041 **EXPECTED FINAL GRAVITY** 1012 **TOTAL LIQUOR** 31.5 LITRES (55½ PINTS)

 MAKES 23 LITRES (40 PINTS)   **READY TO DRINK** 5 WEEKS   **ESTIMATED ABV** 3.8%   **BITTERNESS RATING** 26 IBU   **COLOUR RATING** 7.1 EBC

FOR THE MASH

LIQUOR 11 litres (19½ pints) **MASH TIME** 1 hr **TEMPERATURE** 65°C (149°F)

Grain bill	Quantity
Extra pale malt	4.3kg (9lb 8oz)
Light crystal malt	95g (3⅓oz)

FOR THE BOIL

LIQUOR 27 litres (47½ pints) **BOIL TIME** 1 hr 10 mins

Hops	Quantity	IBU	When to add
Challenger 7%	35g (1¼oz)	26	At start of boil
East Kent Golding 5.5%	23g (¾oz)	0.0	At turn off
Styrian Golding 4.5%	16g (½oz)	0.0	At turn off
Other			
Protofloc	1 tsp		For last 15 mins of boil

TO FERMENT

FERMENTATION 18°C (64°F) **CONDITIONING** 4 weeks at 12°C (54°F)

Yeast
Whitelabs WLP005 English ale

MALT EXTRACT VERSION

Steep 95g (3⅓oz) **crystal malt** in 27 litres (47½ pints) of water at 65°C (149°F) for 30 mins. Remove the malt, then add 2.75kg (6lb 1oz) **dried extra light malt extract**, bring to a boil, and add the hops as specified in the main recipe.

This delicious, strong, and refreshing ale has a crisp, dry finish. The honey imparts a dry rather than sweet flavour, yet still gives the beer a distinct honey character.

Honey Ale

ORIGINAL GRAVITY 1057 **EXPECTED FINAL GRAVITY** 1011 **TOTAL LIQUOR** 34 LITRES (60 PINTS)

 MAKES 23 LITRES (40 PINTS)   **READY TO DRINK** 5 WEEKS   **ESTIMATED ABV** 6.2%   **BITTERNESS RATING** 10 IBU   **COLOUR RATING** 16.2 EBC

FOR THE MASH

LIQUOR 12.5 litres (22 pints) **MASH TIME** 1 hr **TEMPERATURE** 65°C (149°F)

Grain bill	Quantity
Pale malt	4.5kg (10lb)
Biscuit malt	350g (12oz)
Crystal malt	250g (9oz)

FOR THE BOIL

LIQUOR 27 litres (47½ pints) **BOIL TIME** 1 hr 15 mins

Hops	Quantity	IBU	When to add
Challenger 7%	12g (½oz)	9.6	At start of boil
Target 10.5%	8g (¼oz)	0.4	For last 1 min of boil

Other			
Protofloc	1 tsp		For last 15 mins of boil
Honey	500g (1lb 2oz)		For last 5 mins of boil

TO FERMENT

FERMENTATION 18°C (64°F)
CONDITIONING 4 weeks at 12°C (54°F)

Yeast
Danstar Nottingham ale B

MALT EXTRACT VERSION

Steep 350g (12oz) **biscuit malt** and 250g (9oz) **crystal malt** in 27 litres (47½ pints) of water at 65°C (149°F) for 30 mins. Remove the malt, then add 2.85kg (6lb 4oz) **dried light malt extract**, bring to a boil, and add the hops as specified in the main recipe.

Traditionally known as "Fraoch", heather ale has been brewed in Scotland since 2000BCE. It is a lovely golden ale with a herbal, grassy aroma and slightly spicy finish.

Heather Ale

ORIGINAL GRAVITY 1051 EXPECTED FINAL GRAVITY 1014 TOTAL LIQUOR 32.5 LITRES (57 PINTS)

 MAKES 23 LITRES (40 PINTS)   **READY TO DRINK** 5 WEEKS   **ESTIMATED ABV** 4.9%   **BITTERNESS RATING** 25 IBU   **COLOUR RATING** 15.9 EBC

FOR THE MASH

LIQUOR 12.7 litres (22⅓ pints) **MASH TIME** 1 hr **TEMPERATURE** 65°C (149°F)

Grain bill	Quantity
Pale malt	4.34kg (9lb 9oz)
Caramalt	500g (1lb 2oz)
Crystal wheat malt	200g (7oz)

FOR THE BOIL

LIQUOR 27 litres (47½ pints) **BOIL TIME** 1 hr 10 mins

Hops	Quantity	IBU	When to add
Golding 5.5%	41g (1½oz)	2.5	At start of boil
Golding 5.5%	20g (⅔oz)	0.0	At turn off

Other			
Fresh heather tips	75g (2½oz)		At start of boil
Protofloc	1 tsp		For last 15 mins of boil
Fresh heather tips	75g (2½oz)		At turn off

TO FERMENT

FERMENTATION 18°C (64°F) **CONDITIONING** 4 weeks at 12°C (54°F)

Yeast
Whitelabs WLP028 Edinburgh ale

MALT EXTRACT VERSION

Steep 500g (1lb 2oz) **Caramalt** and 200g (7oz) **crystal wheat malt** in 27 litres (47½ pints) of water at 65°C (149°F) for 30 mins. Remove the malt, then add 2.8kg (6lb 3oz) **dried light malt extract**, bring to a boil, and add the hops as specified in the main recipe.

BREWER'S TIP
Try adding 20g (⅔oz) bog myrtle (a deciduous shrub also known as sweet gale) at turn off to add a bittersweet, resinous character to the beer.

Lighter than its cousins Dubbel and Tripel (see pp156–57), Belgian Pale Ale is an easy-drinking beer. The pale malts and light hop varieties create a perfect flavour balance.

Belgian Pale Ale

ORIGINAL GRAVITY 1051 **EXPECTED FINAL GRAVITY** 1013 **TOTAL LIQUOR** 32.5 LITRES (57 PINTS)

 MAKES 23 LITRES (40 PINTS)

 READY TO DRINK 5 WEEKS

 ESTIMATED ABV 5.1%

 BITTERNESS RATING 25 IBU

 COLOUR RATING 16.7 EBC

FOR THE MASH

LIQUOR 12.8 litres (22½ pints) **MASH TIME** 1 hr **TEMPERATURE** 65°C (149°F)

Grain bill	Quantity
Belgian pale malt	4.6kg (10lb 2oz)
Caramunich I	500g (1lb 2oz)

FOR THE BOIL

LIQUOR 27 litres (47½ pints) **BOIL TIME** 1 hr 10 mins

Hops	Quantity	IBU	When to add
Golding 5.5%	38g (1¼oz)	22.9	At start of boil
Saaz 4.2%	13g (½oz)	2.1	For last 10 mins of boil
Saaz 4.2%	38g (1¼oz)	0.0	At turn off
Other			
Protofloc	1 tsp		For last 15 mins of boil

TO FERMENT

FERMENTATION 20°C (68°F) **CONDITIONING** 4 weeks at 12°C (54°F)

Yeast
Wyeast 3522 Belgian Ardennes

MALT EXTRACT VERSION

Steep 500g (1lb 2oz) **Caramunich I malt** in 27 litres (47½ pints) of water at 65°C (149°F) for 30 mins. Remove the malt, then add 2.9kg (6lb 6oz) **dried light malt extract**, bring to a boil, and add the hops as specified in the main recipe.

BREWER'S TIP
To produce a fruitier-flavoured beer, try changing the yeast to Wyeast 3942 Belgian wheat.

Originally brewed as a summer beer in the French-speaking region of Belgium, Saison is a refreshing, spicy ale with strong citrus notes.

Saison

ORIGINAL GRAVITY 1051 **EXPECTED FINAL GRAVITY** 1010 **TOTAL LIQUOR** 32 LITRES (56 PINTS)

 MAKES 23 LITRES (40 PINTS)   **READY TO DRINK** 5 WEEKS   **ESTIMATED ABV** 5.6%   **BITTERNESS RATING** 16 IBU   **COLOUR RATING** 17.1 EBC

FOR THE MASH

LIQUOR 12.3 litres (21½ pints) **MASH TIME** 1 hr **TEMPERATURE** 65°C (149°F)

Grain bill	Quantity
Pilsner malt	3.57kg (7lb 14oz)
Munich malt	890g (2lb)
Wheat malt	180g (6¼oz)
Special B	135g (4¾oz)
Caramunich II	135g (4¾oz)

FOR THE BOIL

LIQUOR 27 litres (47½ pints) **BOIL TIME** 1 hr 10 mins

Hops	Quantity	IBU	When to add
Magnum 11%	13g (½oz)	16.4	At start of boil
Styrian Golding Celeia 5.5%	20g (⅔oz)	0.0	At turn off

Other			
Protofloc	1 tsp		For last 15 mins of boil
Honey	200g (7oz)		For last 5 mins of boil

TO FERMENT

FERMENTATION 24°C (75°F) **CONDITIONING** 4 weeks at 12°C (54°F)

Yeast
Wyeast 3724 Belgian saison

BREWER'S TIP
To ensure proper attenuation (conversion of sugar to alcohol), increase the fermentation temperature to 28°C (82°F) after 4 days.

Traditionally brewed by Belgian monks for personal consumption, Patersbier ("Father's Beer") is a simple, light, and surprisingly flavoursome brew.

QUICK BREW

Patersbier

ORIGINAL GRAVITY 1046 **EXPECTED FINAL GRAVITY** 1010 **TOTAL LIQUOR** 31.5 LITRES (55½ PINTS)

| **MAKES** 23 LITRES (40 PINTS) | **READY TO DRINK** 4 WEEKS | **ESTIMATED ABV** 4.7% | **BITTERNESS RATING** 16.4 IBU | **COLOUR RATING** 5.7 EBC |

FOR THE MASH

LIQUOR 11.25 litres (20 pints) **MASH TIME** 1 hr **TEMPERATURE** 65°C (149°F)

Grain bill	Quantity
Belgian Pilsner malt	4.5kg (10lb)

FOR THE BOIL

LIQUOR 27 litres (47½ pints) **BOIL TIME** 1 hr 10 mins

Hops	Quantity	IBU	When to add
Saaz 4.2%	30g (1oz)	14.4	At start of boil
Hallertauer Mittelfrüh 5%	10g (⅓oz)	2.0	For last 10 mins of boil
Other			
Protofloc	1 tsp		For last 15 mins of boil

TO FERMENT

FERMENTATION 22°C (72°F) **CONDITIONING** 3 weeks at 12°C (54°F)

Yeast
Wyeast 3787 Trappist high gravity

BREWER'S TIP

Try using Saaz hops for both additions during the boil. This will give your brew a slightly more floral aroma.

MALT EXTRACT VERSION

Add 2.9kg (6lb 6oz) **dried light malt extract** to 27 litres (47½ pints) of water, bring to a boil, and add the hops as specified in the main recipe.

In this brew, a light, smoky aroma from the beech-smoked malt is complemented by citrus notes from the American hops and a clean finish from the yeast.

Smoked Beer

ORIGINAL GRAVITY 1051 **EXPECTED FINAL GRAVITY** 1012 **TOTAL LIQUOR** 32 LITRES (56 PINTS)

 MAKES 23 LITRES (40 PINTS)

 READY TO DRINK 6 WEEKS

 ESTIMATED ABV 5.1%

 BITTERNESS RATING 30.2 IBU

COLOUR RATING 23.6 EBC

FOR THE MASH

LIQUOR 12.7 litres (22⅓ pints) **MASH TIME** 1 hr **TEMPERATURE** 65°C (149°F)

Grain bill	Quantity
Pale malt	4kg (8lb 13oz)
Smoked malt	700g (1lb 8oz)
Crystal	300g (10½oz)
Carafa special II	70g (2½oz)

FOR THE BOIL

LIQUOR 27 litres (47½ pints) **BOIL TIME** 1 hr 10 mins

Hops	Quantity	IBU	When to add
Chinook 13.3%	18g (⅔oz)	25.9	At start of boil
Willamette 6.3%	18g (⅔oz)	4.3	For last 15 mins of boil
Willamette 6.3%	18g (⅔oz)	0.0	At turn off

Other			
Protofloc	1 tsp		For last 15 mins of boil

TO FERMENT

FERMENTATION 18°C (64°F) **CONDITIONING** 4 weeks at 12°C (54°F)

Yeast
Wyeast 1056 American ale

BREWER'S TIP

For an authentic barrel-aged character, try adding 100g (3½oz) oak chips to the fermenter after 3 days and leave for 1 week before removing.

First brewed in England in the 19th century for export, the high alcohol content and hop levels in IPA (India Pale Ale) helped preserve the beer on long sea voyages.

English IPA

ORIGINAL GRAVITY 1060 **EXPECTED FINAL GRAVITY** 1017 **TOTAL LIQUOR** 33 LITRES (58 PINTS)

 MAKES
23 LITRES
(40 PINTS)

 READY TO DRINK
5 WEEKS

 ESTIMATED ABV
5.7%

 BITTERNESS RATING
60.1 IBU

  COLOUR RATING
13 EBC

FOR THE MASH

LIQUOR 13.9 litres (24½ pints) **MASH TIME** 1 hr **TEMPERATURE** 65°C (149°F)

Grain bill	Quantity
Pale malt	5.8kg (12lb 9oz)
Crystal malt	145g (5oz)

FOR THE BOIL

LIQUOR 27 litres (47½ pints) **BOIL TIME** 1hr 10mins

Hops	Quantity	IBU	When to add
Challenger 7%	70g (2½oz)	50.5	At start of boil
Golding 5.5%	35g (1¼oz)	9.5	For last 15 mins of boil
Golding 5.5%	35g (1¼oz)	0.0	At turn off

Other			
Protofloc	1 tsp		For last 15 mins of boil

TO FERMENT

FERMENTATION 18°C (64°F) **CONDITIONING** 4 weeks at 12°C (54°F)

Yeast
Wyeast 1187 Ringwood ale

BREWER'S TIP

After 4 days, increase the temperature by 1°C (1.8°F) per day up to 22°C (72°F). This will help achieve the correct attenuation (conversion of sugar to alcohol).

MALT EXTRACT VERSION

Steep 145g (5oz) **crystal malt** in 27 litres (47½ pints) of water at 65°C (149°F) for 30 mins. Remove the malt, then add 3.7kg (8lb 2oz) **dried light malt extract**, bring to a boil, and add the hops as specified in the main recipe.

Multiple hoppings with three different hop varieties give this IPA a powerful, complex, yet well-balanced flavour and aroma – definitely one for the "hop-heads".

60-Minute IPA

ORIGINAL GRAVITY 1055 **EXPECTED FINAL GRAVITY** 1013 **TOTAL LIQUOR** 33 LITRES (58 PINTS)

 MAKES
23 LITRES
(40 PINTS)

 READY TO DRINK
7 WEEKS

  ESTIMATED ABV
5.7%

  BITTERNESS RATING
60 IBU

 COLOUR RATING
6.5 EBC

FOR THE MASH

LIQUOR 14 litres (24½ pints) **MASH TIME** 1 hr **TEMPERATURE** 65°C (149°F)

Grain bill	Quantity
Pale malt (low colour)	5.5kg (12lb 2oz)

FOR THE BOIL

LIQUOR 27 litres (47½ pints) **BOIL TIME** 1 hr

Hops	Quantity	IBU	When to add
Chinook 13.3%	7g (¼oz)	8.9	At start of boil
Amarillo 5%	7g (¼oz)	3.4	At start of boil
Chinook 13.3%	7g (¼oz)	6.9	For last 30 mins of boil
Amarillo 5%	7g (¼oz)	2.6	For last 30 mins of boil
Cascade 6.6%	7g (¼oz)	3.4	For last 30 mins of boil

Then 7g (¼oz) each of Chinook, Amarillo, and Cascade every 5 mins until 1 hr is up

Hops	Quantity	IBU	When to add
Chinook 13.3%	10g (⅓oz)	0.0	At turn off
Amarillo 5%	10g (⅓oz)	0.0	At turn off
Cascade 6.6%	10g (⅓oz)	0.0	At turn off

Other			
Protofloc	1 tsp		For last 15 mins of boil

TO FERMENT

FERMENTATION 18°C (64°F) **CONDITIONING** 6 weeks at 12°C (54°F)

Yeast
Whitelabs WLP001 California ale

MALT EXTRACT VERSION

Add 3.5kg (7lb 11oz) **dried extra light malt extract** to 27 litres (47½ pints) of water, bring to a boil, and add the hops as specified in the main recipe.

This brew has all the hallmarks of a classic American IPA – a hoppy bitterness, balanced by a relatively high alcohol content, and a powerful citrus aroma.

American IPA

ORIGINAL GRAVITY 1060 **EXPECTED FINAL GRAVITY** 1014 **TOTAL LIQUOR** 34 LITRES (60 PINTS)

 MAKES 23 LITRES (40 PINTS)   **READY TO DRINK** 7 WEEKS   **ESTIMATED ABV** 6.2%   **BITTERNESS RATING** 55 IBU   **COLOUR RATING** 10.6 EBC

FOR THE MASH

LIQUOR 15 litres (26 pints) **MASH TIME** 1 hr **TEMPERATURE** 65°C (149°F)

Grain bill	Quantity
Pale malt	6kg (13lb 4oz)

FOR THE BOIL

LIQUOR 27 litres (47½ pints) **BOIL TIME** 1 hr 10 mins

Hops	Quantity	IBU	When to add
Citra 13.8%	29g (1oz)	40.9	At start of boil
Citra 13.8%	15g (½oz)	7.2	For last 10 mins of boil
Simcoe 13%	15g (½oz)	6.8	For last 10 mins of boil
Citra 13.8%	44g (1½oz)	0.0	At turn off
Simcoe 13%	44g (1½oz)	0.0	At turn off

Other			
Protofloc	1 tsp		For last 15 mins of boil

TO FERMENT

FERMENTATION 18°C (64°F) **CONDITIONING** 6 weeks at 12°C (54°F)

Yeast
Whitelabs WLP060 American ale blend

MALT EXTRACT VERSION

Add 3.75kg (8lb 4oz) **dried light malt extract** to 27 litres (47½ pints) of water, bring to a boil, and add the hops as specified in the main recipe.

This beer is deceptively strong as the high levels of alcohol are balanced by a hop bitterness, sweet malt flavours, and a fresh, citrus aroma.

Imperial IPA

ORIGINAL GRAVITY 1083 **EXPECTED FINAL GRAVITY** 1018 **TOTAL LIQUOR** 36 LITRES (63 PINTS)

 MAKES 23 LITRES (40 PINTS)   **READY TO DRINK** 13 WEEKS   **ESTIMATED ABV** 8.6%   **BITTERNESS RATING** 75 IBU   **COLOUR RATING** 24 EBC

FOR THE MASH

LIQUOR 21 litres (37 pints) **MASH TIME** 1 hr **TEMPERATURE** 65°C (149°F)

Grain bill	Quantity
Pale malt	8.1kg (17lb 14oz)
Light crystal malt (60L)	100g (3½oz)
Chocolate malt	80g (2¾oz)

FOR THE BOIL

LIQUOR 27 litres (47½ pints) **BOIL TIME** 1 hr 10 mins

Hops	Quantity	IBU	When to add
Chinook 13.3%	56g (2oz)	64.0	At start of boil
Simcoe 13%	28g (1oz)	11.0	For last 10 mins of boil
Simcoe 13%	50g (1¾oz)	0.0	At turn off
Willamette 6.3%	50g (1¾oz)	0.0	At turn off

Other			
Protofloc	1 tsp		Fot last 15 mins of boil

TO FERMENT

FERMENTATION 20°C (68°F) **CONDITIONING** 12 weeks at 12°C (54°F)

Yeast
Whitelabs WLP001 California ale

Hops	Quantity	IBU	When to add
Willamette 6.3%	50g (1¾oz)	0.0	Dry hop after 4 days

MALT EXTRACT VERSION

Steep 100g (3½oz) **light crystal malt (60L)** and 80g (2¾oz) **chocolate malt** in 27 litres (47½ pints) of water at 65°C (149°F) for 30 mins. Remove the malt, then add 5.1kg (1lb 4oz) **dried light malt extract**, bring to a boil, and add the hops as specified in the main recipe.

As black as night but with the clean, citrus finish you would expect from a pale or golden ale, the contradiction in this beer will confuse the senses but delight the palate.

Black IPA

ORIGINAL GRAVITY 1054 **EXPECTED FINAL GRAVITY** 1018 **TOTAL LIQUOR** 33 LITRES (58 PINTS)

 MAKES 23 LITRES (40 PINTS)　 **READY TO DRINK** 7 WEEKS　 **ESTIMATED ABV** 5.1%　 **BITTERNESS RATING** 60 IBU　 **COLOUR RATING** 56 EBC

FOR THE MASH

LIQUOR 13.5 litres (23¾ pints) **MASH TIME** 1 hr **TEMPERATURE** 65°C (149°F)

Grain bill	Quantity
Pale malt	5.5kg (12lb 2oz)
Carafa special III	170g (6oz)
Chocolate malt	225g (8oz)

FOR THE BOIL

LIQUOR 27 litres (47½ pints) **BOIL TIME** 1 hr 10 mins

Hops	Quantity	IBU	When to add
Apollo 19.5%	30g (1oz)	44.0	At start of boil
Citra 13.8%	30g (1oz)	16.0	For last 10 mins of boil
Amarillo 5%	45g (1½oz)	0.0	At turn off
Citra 13.8%	45g (1½oz)	0.0	At turn off

Other			
Protofloc	1 tsp		For last 15 mins of boil

TO FERMENT

FERMENTATION 18°C (64°F) **CONDITIONING** 6 weeks at 12°C (54°F)

Yeast
Wyeast 1187 Ringwood ale

Hops	Quantity	IBU	When to add
Citra 13.8%	45g (1½oz)	0.0	Dry hop after 4 days

MALT EXTRACT VERSION

Steep 170g (6oz) **Carafa special III malt** and 225g (8oz) **chocolate malt** in 27 litres (47½ pints) of water at 65°C (149°F) for 30 mins. Remove the malt, then add 3.15kg (7lb) **dried malt extract**, bring to a boil, and add the hops as specified in the main recipe.

A long ageing process is needed to fully develop the flavours in this complex, sour, and fruity beer – once bottled, wait for at least a year before sampling.

Flanders Red Ale

ORIGINAL GRAVITY 1056 **EXPECTED FINAL GRAVITY** 1010 **TOTAL LIQUOR** 33 LITRES (58 PINTS)

 MAKES 23 LITRES (40 PINTS)
 READY TO DRINK 1+ YEARS
  ESTIMATED ABV 6.2%
 BITTERNESS RATING 20.7 IBU
 COLOUR RATING 29 EBC

FOR THE MASH

LIQUOR 14 litres (24½ pints) **MASH TIME** 1 hr **TEMPERATURE** 65°C (149°F)

Grain bill	Quantity
Vienna malt	3.2kg (7lb 1oz)
Pale malt	1.6kg (3lb 8oz)
Wheat malt	250g (9oz)
Special B	300g (10½oz)
Caramunich III	300g (10½oz)

FOR THE BOIL

LIQUOR 27 litres (47½ pints) **BOIL TIME** 1 hr 10 mins

Hops	Quantity	IBU	When to add
East Kent Golding 5.5%	36g (1¼oz)	20.7	At start of boil
Other			
Protofloc	1 tsp		For last 15 mins of boil

TO FERMENT

FERMENTATION at least 4 weeks at 22°C (72°F) **CONDITIONING** at least 6 months at 22°C (72°F)

Yeast
Wyeast 3763 Roselare Belgian blend

BREWER'S TIP

Try adding a little fresh fruit to the conditioning fermenter after 3 months. Cherries or raspberries are a good choice.

Lambic is a traditional Belgian style of sour beer. Most of the flavour profiles come from the wild yeast strains, which are added after primary fermentation.

Cherry Lambic

ORIGINAL GRAVITY 1060 **EXPECTED FINAL GRAVITY** 1005 **TOTAL LIQUOR** 34 LITRES (60 PINTS)

 MAKES 23 LITRES (40 PINTS)
 READY TO DRINK 10 WEEKS
 ESTIMATED ABV 7.3%
 BITTERNESS RATING 15 IBU
 COLOUR RATING 10 EBC

FOR THE MASH

LIQUOR 17.5 litres (31 pints) **MASH TIME** 1 hr **TEMPERATURE** 65°C (149°F)

Grain bill	Quantity
Pale malt	4.5kg (10lb)
Wheat malt	1.5kg (3lb 3oz)

FOR THE BOIL

LIQUOR 27 litres (47½ pints) **BOIL TIME** 1 hr 10 mins

Hops	Quantity	IBU	When to add
Challenger 13.3%	30g (1oz)	14.0	At start of boil

Other			
Protofloc	1 tsp		For last 15 mins of boil

TO FERMENT

FERMENTATION 22°C (72°F) for 2 weeks, then add secondary yeast strains and ferment for a further 4 weeks **CONDITIONING** 4 weeks at 12°C (54°F)

Yeast
DCL WB-06, along with 6kg (13lb 4oz) morello cherries

After 2 weeks, add Wyeast 5335 Lactobacillus, Wyeast 5526 Brettanomyces Lambicus, and Wyeast 5733 Pediococcus and leave for a further 4 weeks

BREWER'S TIP
Use a separate, dedicated fermenter for this brew as the wild yeast strains may infect future batches of beer.

MALT EXTRACT VERSION

Add 2kg (4½lb) **dried light malt extract** and 1.7kg (3lb 12oz) **dried wheat malt extract** to 27 litres (47½ pints) of water, bring to a boil, and add the hops as specified in the main recipe.

This tawny coloured classic English bitter achieves a perfect balance between malt and hops. The London yeast creates a moreish, sweet, and slightly fruity finish.

London Bitter

ORIGINAL GRAVITY 1044 **EXPECTED FINAL GRAVITY** 1012 **TOTAL LIQUOR** 32 LITRES (56 PINTS)

 MAKES 23 LITRES (40 PINTS)   **READY TO DRINK** 5 WEEKS   **ESTIMATED ABV** 4.3%   **BITTERNESS RATING** 22.1 IBU   **COLOUR RATING** 17 EBC

FOR THE MASH

LIQUOR 11 litres (19½ pints) **MASH TIME** 1 hr **TEMPERATURE** 65°C (149°F)

Grain bill	Quantity
Pale malt	4kg (8lb 13oz)
Crystal malt	396g (14oz)

FOR THE BOIL

LIQUOR 27 litres (47½ pints) **BOIL TIME** 1 hr 10 mins

Hops	Quantity	IBU	When to add
Challenger 7%	25g (1oz)	20.3	At start of boil
Fuggle 4.5%	10g (⅓oz)	1.8	For last 10 mins of boil
Golding 5.5%	6g (¼oz)	0.0	At turn off
Other			
Protofloc	1 tsp		For last 15 mins of boil

TO FERMENT

FERMENTATION 18°C (64°F) **CONDITIONING** 4 weeks at 12°C (°F)

Yeast
Wyeast 1318 London ale III

MALT EXTRACT VERSION

Steep 396g (14oz) **crystal malt** in 27 litres (47½ pints) of water at 65°C (149°F) for 30 mins. Remove the malt, then add 2.5kg (5½lb) **dried malt extract**, bring to a boil, and add the hops as specified in the main recipe.

BREWER'S TIP

For a less sweet beer, try using just 200g (7oz) crystal malt in the mash and add 30g (1oz) chocolate malt.

A full-bodied amber beer with a subtle chocolate flavour that develops into a pithy bitterness, Yorkshire Bitter is traditionally served with a creamy white head.

Yorkshire Bitter

ORIGINAL GRAVITY 1041 **EXPECTED FINAL GRAVITY** 1012 **TOTAL LIQUOR** 31.5 LITRES (55½ PINTS)

 MAKES 23 LITRES (40 PINTS)

 READY TO DRINK 5 WEEKS

 ESTIMATED ABV 3.8%

 BITTERNESS RATING 31 IBU

 COLOUR RATING 18 EBC

FOR THE MASH

LIQUOR 10.5 litres (18½ pints) **MASH TIME** 1 hr **TEMPERATURE** 65°C (149°F)

Grain bill	Quantity
Pale malt	3.5kg (7lb 11oz)
Crystal malt	200g (7oz)
Torrified wheat	350g (12oz)
Chocolate malt	42g (1½oz)

FOR THE BOIL

LIQUOR 27 litres (47½ pints) **BOIL TIME** 1 hr 10 mins

Hops	Quantity	IBU	When to add
Challenger 7%	29g (1oz)	24.3	At start of boil
First Gold 8%	20g (⅔oz)	6.7	For last 10 mins of boil
First Gold 8%	12g (½oz)	0.0	At turn off
Other			
Protofloc	1 tsp		For last 15 mins of boil

TO FERMENT

FERMENTATION 20°C (68°F) **CONDITIONING** 4 weeks at 12°C (54°F)

Yeast
Wyeast 1469 West Yorkshire ale

MALT EXTRACT VERSION

Steep 200g (7oz) **crystal malt** and 42g (1½oz) **chocolate malt** in 27 litres (47½ pints) of water at 65°C (149°F) for 30 mins. Remove the malt, then add 2kg (4½lb) **dried malt extract** and 450g (1lb) **dried wheat malt extract**, bring to a boil, and add the hops as specified in the main recipe.

BREWER'S TIP

Serve from a barrel using a beer engine (pump) and a swan-neck adapter fitted with a sparklet – this will aerate the beer and produce a creamy head.

A delicious and light session beer for those long summer evenings. Although low in gravity, this ale is packed with flavour and has a wonderful hoppy finish.

Summer Ale

ORIGINAL GRAVITY 1038 **EXPECTED FINAL GRAVITY** 1012 **TOTAL LIQUOR** 31 LITRES (54½ PINTS)

 MAKES 23 LITRES (40 PINTS)   **READY TO DRINK** 5 WEEKS   **ESTIMATED ABV** 3.8%   **BITTERNESS RATING** 29.3 IBU **COLOUR RATING** 13 EBC

FOR THE MASH

LIQUOR 9.5 litres (16½ pints) **MASH TIME** 1 hr **TEMPERATURE** 65°C (149°F)

Grain bill	Quantity
Pale malt	3.4kg (7½lb)
Crystal malt	300g (10½oz)

FOR THE BOIL

LIQUOR 27 litres (47½ pints) **BOIL TIME** 1 hr 10 mins

Hops	Quantity	IBU	When to add
East Kent Golding 5.5%	20g (⅔oz)	9.4	At start of boil
Progress 5.5%	15g (½oz)	7.0	At start of boil
East Kent Golding 5.5%	15g (½oz)	7.5	For last 30 mins of boil
Progress 5.5%	10g (⅓oz)	5.0	For last 30 mins of boil
East Kent Golding 5.5%	15g (½oz)	0.4	For last 1 min of boil
Other			
Protofloc	1 tsp		For last 15 mins of boil

TO FERMENT

FERMENTATION 20°C (68°F) **CONDITIONING** 4 weeks at 12°C (54°F)

Yeast
Wyeast 1098 British ale

MALT EXTRACT VERSION

Steep 300g (10½oz) **crystal malt** in 27 litres (47½ pints) of water at 65°C (149°F) for 30 mins. Remove the malt, then add 2.2kg (4lb 13oz) **dried malt extract**, bring to a boil, and add the hops as specified in the main recipe.

BREWER'S TIP
Store in a barrel, rather than in bottles, and serve with a minimum amount of head for a light, hoppy, easy-drinking pint.

Strong and malty with biscuity undertones and notes of blackcurrent, this is a delicious and satisfying brew to be savoured after a long day at work.

Cornish Tin Miner's Ale

ORIGINAL GRAVITY 1058 **EXPECTED FINAL GRAVITY** 1019 **TOTAL LIQUOR** 33 LITRES (58 PINTS)

 MAKES 23 LITRES (40 PINTS)   **READY TO DRINK** 9 WEEKS   **ESTIMATED ABV** 5.2%   **BITTERNESS RATING** 39.9 IBU   **COLOUR RATING** 19 EBC

FOR THE MASH

LIQUOR 14.5 litres (25½ pints) **MASH TIME** 1 hr **TEMPERATURE** 65°C (149°F)

Grain bill	Quantity
Pale malt	4.9kg (10lb 13oz)
Caramunich	380g (13½oz)
Biscuit malt	250g (9oz)
Crystal malt	185g (6½oz)

FOR THE BOIL

LIQUOR 27 litres (47½ pints) **BOIL TIME** 1 hr 10 mins

Hops	Quantity	IBU	When to add
First Gold 8%	46g (1½oz)	38.0	At start of boil
Bramling Cross 6%	15g (½oz)	3.3	For last 10 mins of boil
Bramling Cross 6%	15g (½oz)	0.0	At turn off
Other			
Protofloc	1 tsp		For last 15 mins of boil

TO FERMENT

FERMENTATION 20°C (68°F) **CONDITIONING** 8 weeks at 12°C (54°F)

Yeast
Whitelabs WLP002 English ale

MALT EXTRACT VERSION

Steep 380g (13½oz) **Caramunich**, 250g (9oz) **biscuit malt**, and 185g (6½oz) **crystal malt** in 27 litres (47½ pints) of water at 65°C (149°F) for 30 mins. Remove the malt, then add 3.15kg (7lb) **dried extra light malt extract**, bring to a boil, and add the hops as specified in the main recipe.

BREWER'S TIP

Try changing the yeast to Whitelabs WLP007 dry English ale for a drier-flavoured version of this brew.

A particularly light-bodied, traditional Scottish session beer, Scottish 60 Shilling is malty and dry with a crisp, clean finish.

Scottish 60 Shilling

ORIGINAL GRAVITY 1035 **EXPECTED FINAL GRAVITY** 1010 **TOTAL LIQUOR** 30.5 LITRES (54 PINTS)

 MAKES 23 LITRES (40 PINTS)

 READY TO DRINK 7 WEEKS

 ESTIMATED ABV 3.3%

 BITTERNESS RATING 11.7 IBU

  COLOUR RATING 18 EBC

FOR THE MASH

LIQUOR 8.6 litres (15¼ pints) **MASH TIME** 1 hr **TEMPERATURE** 70°C (160°F)

Grain bill	Quantity
Pale malt	3kg (6lb 10oz)
Munich malt	175g (6oz)
Crystal malt	130g (4½oz)
Melanoidin malt	100g (3½oz)
Chocolate malt	50g (1¾oz)

FOR THE BOIL

LIQUOR 27 litres (47½ pints) **BOIL TIME** 1 hr 10 mins

Hops	Quantity	IBU	When to add
Fuggle 4.5%	21g (¾oz)	11.6	At start of boil

Other			
Protofloc	1 tsp		For last 15 mins of boil

TO FERMENT

FERMENTATION 18°C (64°F)
CONDITIONING 6 weeks at 12°C (54°F)

Yeast
Wyeast 1728 Scottish ale

Scottish 70 Shilling, also known as "heavy", is a medium-gravity beer with dominant malt flavours and a low hop flavour and aroma.

Scottish 70 Shilling

ORIGINAL GRAVITY 1041 **EXPECTED FINAL GRAVITY** 1012 **TOTAL LIQUOR** 32.5 LITRES (57 PINTS)

 MAKES
23 LITRES
(40 PINTS)

 READY TO DRINK
5 WEEKS

 ESTIMATED ABV
3.9%

 BITTERNESS RATING
15 IBU

 COLOUR RATING
28.2 EBC

FOR THE MASH

LIQUOR 13 litres (23 pints) **MASH TIME** 1 hr **TEMPERATURE** 70°C (160°F)

Grain bill	Quantity
Pale malt	3.5kg (7lb 11oz)
Caramunich II malt	450g (1lb)
Carafa I malt	130g (4½oz)

FOR THE BOIL

LIQUOR 27 litres (47½ pints) **BOIL TIME** 1 hr 15 mins

Hops	Quantity	IBU	When to add
Golding 5.5%	23g (¾oz)	15.0	At start of boil
Other			
Protofloc	1 tsp		For last 15 mins of boil

TO FERMENT

FERMENTATION 18°C (64°F) **CONDITIONING** 4 weeks at 12°C (54°F)

Yeast
Wyeast 1728 Scottish ale

MALT EXTRACT VERSION

Steep 450g (1lb) **Caramunich II malt** and 130g (4½oz) **Carafa I malt** in 27 litres (47½ pints) of water at 65°C (149°F) for 30 mins. Remove the malt, then add 2.55kg (5lb 10oz) **dried light malt extract**, bring to a boil, and add the hops as specified in the main recipe.

10 / 2019 5:43 PM

Item(s) checked out to
D4000000415520 (lost)

The art of living / Thich Nhat Hanh
Date Due: 22 Oct 2019

Home brew beer / Greg Hughes
Date Due: **22 Oct 2019**

To renew your items
Online at libraries.bexhill.com Ph: 01 061 0412
Mon-Thurs 9:45am-8pm Fri/Sat 9:45am-4:00pm

Paperless overdues coming soon!

From December 1st we will no longer post overdue
notices. Please sign up to receive email notices via
your online library account

Like many other Scottish beers, Scottish 80 Shilling is very malty, with no hop aroma, but has a clean, neutral finish. This is an "export" strength Scottish classic.

Scottish 80 Shilling

ORIGINAL GRAVITY 1052 **EXPECTED FINAL GRAVITY** 1015 **TOTAL LIQUOR** 32.5 LITRES (57 PINTS)

 MAKES 23 LITRES (40 PINTS)   **READY TO DRINK** 7 WEEKS   **ESTIMATED ABV** 4.9%   **BITTERNESS RATING** 16.5 IBU   **COLOUR RATING** 29.2 EBC

FOR THE MASH

LIQUOR 13 litres (23 pints) **MASH TIME** 1 hr **TEMPERATURE** 70°C (160°F)

Grain bill	Quantity
Pale malt	4.6kg (10lb 2oz)
Caramunich II malt	300g (10½oz)
Crystal malt	200g (7oz)
Carafa III malt	80g (2¾oz)

FOR THE BOIL

LIQUOR 27 litres (47½ pints) **BOIL TIME** 1 hr 10 mins

Hops	Quantity	IBU	When to add
Golding 5.5%	27g (1oz)	16.5	At start of boil
Other			
Protofloc	1 tsp		For last 15 mins of boil

TO FERMENT

FERMENTATION 18°C (64°F) **CONDITIONING** 6 weeks at 12°C (54°F)

Yeast
Wyeast 1728 Scottish ale

MALT EXTRACT VERSION

Steep 300g (10½oz) **Caramunich II malt**, 200g (7oz) **crystal malt**, and 80g (2¾oz) **Carafa III malt** in 27 litres (47½ pints) of water at 65°C (149°F) for 30 mins. Remove the malt, then add 2.9kg (6lb 6oz) **dried light malt extract**, bring to a boil, and add the hops as specified in the main recipe.

Closely related in style to English bitter, Irish Red Ale is a refreshing, lightly hopped beer with a malty flavour, clean finish, and distinctive red hue.

Irish Red Ale

ORIGINAL GRAVITY 1051 EXPECTED FINAL GRAVITY 1013 TOTAL LIQUOR 32.5 LITRES (57 PINTS)

 MAKES 23 LITRES (40 PINTS)   **READY TO DRINK** 7 WEEKS   **ESTIMATED ABV** 5.0%   **BITTERNESS RATING** 24.5 IBU   **COLOUR RATING** 23 EBC

FOR THE MASH

LIQUOR 12.8 litres (22½ pints) **MASH TIME** 1 hr **TEMPERATURE** 65°C (149°F)

Grain bill	Quantity
Pale malt	4.6kg (10lb 2oz)
Crystal malt	200g (7oz)
Flaked barley	300g (10½oz)
Roasted barley	50g (1¾oz)

FOR THE BOIL

LIQUOR 27 litres (47½ pints) **BOIL TIME** 1 hr 10 mins

Hops	Quantity	IBU	When to add
Fuggle 4.5%	50g (1¾oz)	24.5	At start of boil
Challenger 7%	33g (1¼oz)	0.0	At turn off

Other			
Protofloc	1 tsp		For last 15 mins of boil

TO FERMENT

FERMENTATION 20°C (68°F)
CONDITIONING 6 weeks at 12°C (54°F)

Yeast
Wyeast 1084 Irish ale

Traditionally brewed in autumn to take advantage of the bounty of malts from the grain harvest, spices can be added to this delicious winter beer for a festive treat.

Winter Warmer

ORIGINAL GRAVITY 1062 **EXPECTED FINAL GRAVITY** 1015 **TOTAL LIQUOR** 32.5 LITRES (57 PINTS)

 MAKES 23 LITRES (40 PINTS)

 READY TO DRINK 8 WEEKS

 ESTIMATED ABV 6.2%

 BITTERNESS RATING 19.6 IBU

 COLOUR RATING 27.2 EBC

FOR THE MASH

LIQUOR 13.75 litres (24¼ pints) **MASH TIME** 1 hr **TEMPERATURE** 65°C (149°F)

Grain bill	Quantity
Pale malt	5.1kg (11lb 4oz)
Crystal malt	200g (7oz)
Torrified wheat malt	100g (3½oz)
Chocolate malt	100g (3½oz)

FOR THE BOIL

LIQUOR 27 litres (47½ pints) **BOIL TIME** 1 hr 10 mins

Hops	Quantity	IBU	When to add
East Kent Golding 5.5%	30g (1oz)	17.5	At start of boil
Progress 5.5%	10g (⅓oz)	2.1	For last 10 mins of boil
Target 10.5%	10g (⅓oz)	0.0	At turn off

Other			
Protofloc	1 tsp		For last 15 mins of boil
Honey	500g (1lb 2oz)		For last 5 mins of boil

TO FERMENT

FERMENTATION 20°C (68°F) **CONDITIONING** 6 weeks at 12°C (54°F)

Yeast
Wyeast 1968 London ESB

MALT EXTRACT VERSION

Steep 200g (7oz) **crystal malt** and 100g (3½oz) **chocolate malt** in 27 litres (47½ pints) of water at 65°C (149°F) for 30 mins. Remove the malt, then add 3.3kg (7lb 4oz) **light dried malt extract**, bring to a boil, and add the hops as specified in the main recipe.

BREWER'S TIP
After 4 days, steep 1 tsp cinnamon and 1 tbsp grated ginger in 50ml (2fl oz) vodka for 15 mins, then add this mixture to the fermenter for 1 week before bottling.

A dark and malty festive brew with a subtle hint of Christmas spices, this strong, special beer should be left to mature for three months before being savoured.

Christmas Ale

ORIGINAL GRAVITY 1063 **EXPECTED FINAL GRAVITY** 1012 **TOTAL LIQUOR** 32.5 LITRES (57 PINTS)

 MAKES 23 LITRES (40 PINTS)   **READY TO DRINK** 12 WEEKS   **ESTIMATED ABV** 6.8%   **BITTERNESS RATING** 25 IBU   **COLOUR RATING** 30.7 EBC

FOR THE MASH

LIQUOR 14 litres (24½ pints) **MASH TIME** 1 hr **TEMPERATURE** 67°C (149°F)

Grain bill	Quantity
Pale malt	4.4kg (9lb 11oz)
Biscuit malt	500g (1lb 2oz)
Caramunich I	350g (12oz)
Crystal malt	300g (10½oz)
Torrified wheat malt	100g (3½oz)
Carafa special I malt	100g (3½oz)

FOR THE BOIL

LIQUOR 27 litres (47½ pints) **BOIL TIME** 1 hr 10 mins

Hops	Quantity	IBU	When to add
Challenger 7%	18g (⅔oz)	13.2	At start of boil
Styrian Golding 4.5%	26g (1oz)	5.9	For last 15 mins of boil
Styrian Golding 4.5%	26g (1oz)	0.0	At turn off

Other			
Protofloc	1 tsp		For last 15 mins of boil
Star anise	10g (⅓oz)		For last 10 mins of boil
Cinnamon sticks	2 sticks		For last 10 mins of boil
Ground nutmeg	1 tsp		For last 10 mins of boil
Light candi crystals	500g (1lb 2oz)		For last 5 mins of boil

TO FERMENT

FERMENTATION 22°C (72°F) **CONDITIONING** 8 weeks at 12°C (54°F)

Yeast
Wyeast 1028 London ale

An artisan farmhouse ale from northern France, this "beer for keeping" was traditionally brewed in early spring and lagered until the summer. It has a lovely, malty sweetness.

Bière de Garde

ORIGINAL GRAVITY 1065   **EXPECTED FINAL GRAVITY** 1014   **TOTAL LIQUOR** 32 LITRES (56 PINTS)

MAKES 23 LITRES (40 PINTS)	**READY TO DRINK** 7 WEEKS	**ESTIMATED ABV** 7%	**BITTERNESS RATING** 25 IBU	**COLOUR RATING** 17.7 EBC

FOR THE MASH

LIQUOR 18.4 litres (32⅓ pints)   **MASH TIME** 1 hr   **TEMPERATURE** 65°C (149°F)

Grain bill	Quantity
Pale malt	4kg (8lb 13oz)
Vienna malt	1.5kg (3lb 3oz)
Aromatic malt	500g (1lb 2oz)
Biscuit malt	500g (1lb 2oz)

FOR THE BOIL

LIQUOR 27 litres (47½ pints)   **BOIL TIME** 1 hr 10 mins

Hops	Quantity	IBU	When to add
Brewers Gold 7%	33g (1¼oz)	22.9	At start of boil
Tettnang 4.5%	25g (1oz)	2.1	For last 5 mins of boil
Tettnang 4.5%	25g (1oz)	0.0	At turn off

Other			
Protofloc	1 tsp		For last 15 mins of boil

TO FERMENT

FERMENTATION 22°C (72°F)   **CONDITIONING** 6 weeks at 12°C (54°F)

Yeast
Wyeast 3711 French saison

Traditionally, each Belgian monastery created its own unique style of high-quality beer. This example has a complex malty flavour with spicy alcohol notes.

Abbey Beer

ORIGINAL GRAVITY 1060 **EXPECTED FINAL GRAVITY** 1013 **TOTAL LIQUOR** 33 LITRES (58 PINTS)

 MAKES 23 LITRES (40 PINTS)

 READY TO DRINK 7 WEEKS

 ESTIMATED ABV 6.4%

 BITTERNESS RATING 19.8 IBU

COLOUR RATING 12.1 EBC

FOR THE MASH

LIQUOR 15 litres (26 pints) **MASH TIME** 1 hr **TEMPERATURE** 65°C (149°F)

Grain bill	Quantity
Belgian Pilsner malt	4.5kg (10lb)
Vienna malt	1kg (2¼lb)
Biscuit malt	500g (1lb 2oz)

FOR THE BOIL

LIQUOR 27 litres (47½ pints) **BOIL TIME** 1 hr 15 mins

Hops	Quantity	IBU	When to add
Perle 8%	21g (¾oz)	17.5	At start of boil
Styrian Golding 5.5%	21g (¾oz)	2.3	For last 5 mins of boil

Other			
Protofloc	1 tsp		For last 15 mins of boil

TO FERMENT

FERMENTATION 22°C (72°F)
CONDITIONING 6 weeks at 12°C (54°F)

Yeast
Wyeast 1214 Belgian ale

A strong, straw-coloured ale originating from Belgium, the malty sweetness in this brew is complemented by a spicy, slightly hoppy aroma and a dry, candi-sugar finish.

Belgian Blonde Ale

ORIGINAL GRAVITY 1070 EXPECTED FINAL GRAVITY 1015 TOTAL LIQUOR 33.5 LITRES (59 PINTS)

 MAKES 23 LITRES (40 PINTS)   **READY TO DRINK** 8 WEEKS   **ESTIMATED ABV** 7.4%   **BITTERNESS RATING** 18 IBU   **COLOUR RATING** 12.9 EBC

FOR THE MASH

LIQUOR 16.25 litres (28½ pints) **MASH TIME** 1 hr **TEMPERATURE** 65°C (149°F)

Grain bill	Quantity
Pilsner malt	6kg (13lb 4oz)
Cara Vienna malt	250g (9oz)
Caramunich I malt	250g (9oz)

FOR THE BOIL

LIQUOR 27 litres (47½ pints) **BOIL TIME** 1 hr 10 mins

Hops	Quantity	IBU	When to add
East Kent Golding 5.5%	30g (1oz)	16.1	At start of boil
Styrian Golding 5.5%	10g (⅓oz)	1.9	For last 10 mins of boil
Styrian Golding 5.5%	20g (⅔oz)	1.9	At turn off

Other			
Protofloc	1 tsp		For last 15 mins of boil
Belgian candi sugar light	300g (10½oz)		For last 5 mins of boil

TO FERMENT

FERMENTATION 22°C (72°F) **CONDITIONING** 6 weeks at 12°C (54°F)

Yeast
Wyeast 1388 Belgian strong

MALT EXTRACT VERSION

Steep 250g (9oz) **Cara Vienna malt** and 250g (9oz) **Caramunich I malt** in 27 litres (47½ pints) of water at 65°C (149°F) for 30 mins. Remove the malt, then add 3.8kg (8lb 6oz) **dried extra light malt extract**, bring to a boil, and add the hops as specified in the main recipe.

A complex, malty sweetness combined with moderate fruitiness make this Belgian classic a real delight. It is strong, deep red in colour, and has a lovely, spicy flavour.

Belgian Dubbel

ORIGINAL GRAVITY 1066 EXPECTED FINAL GRAVITY 1014 TOTAL LIQUOR 33 LITRES (58 PINTS)

 MAKES 23 LITRES (40 PINTS)   **READY TO DRINK** 8 WEEKS   **ESTIMATED ABV** 6.9%   **BITTERNESS RATING** 20.5 IBU   **COLOUR RATING** 29.2 EBC

FOR THE MASH

LIQUOR 15 litres (26 pints) **MASH TIME** 1 hr **TEMPERATURE** 65°C (149°F)

Grain bill	Quantity
Belgian Pilsner malt	5.3kg (11lb 11oz)
Special B malt	400g (14oz)
Caramunich I malt	300g (10½oz)

FOR THE BOIL

LIQUOR 27 litres (47½ pints) **BOIL TIME** 1 hr 10 mins

Hops	Quantity	IBU	When to add
Hallertauer Hersbrucker 3.5%	35g (1¼oz)	12.7	At start of boil
Tettnang 4.5%	35g (1¼oz)	7.5	For last 15 mins of boil
Other			
Protofloc	1 tsp		For last 15 mins of boil
Belgian light candi crystals	400g (14oz)		For last 5 mins of boil

TO FERMENT

FERMENTATION 22°C (72°F) **CONDITIONING** 7 weeks at 12°C (54°F)

Yeast
Wyeast 3944 Belgian witbier

MALT EXTRACT VERSION

Steep 400g (14oz) **Special B malt** and 300g (10½oz) **Caramunich I malt** in 27 litres (47½ pints) of water at 65°C (149°F) for 30 mins. Remove the malt, then add 3.4kg (7½lb) **dried extra light malt extract**, bring to a boil, and add the hops and other ingredients as specified in the main recipe.

With less complex malt flavours than its cousin Dubbel (see opposite), Belgian Tripel has a crisp, tart finish. Although high in alcohol, it doesn't taste overpowering.

Belgian Tripel

ORIGINAL GRAVITY 1080 **EXPECTED FINAL GRAVITY** 1013 **TOTAL LIQUOR** 33.5 LITRES (59 PINTS)

 MAKES
23 LITRES
(40 PINTS)

 READY TO DRINK
12 WEEKS

 ESTIMATED ABV
9.1%

 BITTERNESS RATING
30.2 IBU

 COLOUR RATING
11.4 EBC

FOR THE MASH

LIQUOR 16.3 litres (28⅔ pints) **MASH TIME** 1 hr **TEMPERATURE** 65°C (149°F)

Grain bill	Quantity
Belgian Pilsner malt	6.3kg (14lb)
Caramunich I malt	250g (9oz)

FOR THE BOIL

LIQUOR 27 litres (47½ pints) **BOIL TIME** 1 hr 10 mins

Hops	Quantity	IBU	When to add
Saaz 4.2%	50g (1¾oz)	18.6	At start of boil
Styrian Golding 5.5%	50g (1¾oz)	11.7	For last 15 mins of boil

Other			
Protofloc	1 tsp		For last 15 mins of boil
Belgian light candi crystals	1kg (2¼lb)		For last 5 mins of boil

TO FERMENT

FERMENTATION 24°C (75°F) **CONDITIONING** 11 weeks at 12°C (54°F)

Yeast
Wyeast 1388 Belgian strong ale

MALT EXTRACT VERSION

Steep 250g (9oz) **Caramunich I malt** in 27 litres (47½ pints) of water at 65°C (149°F) for 30 mins. Remove the malt, then add 4kg (8lb 13oz) **dried extra light malt extract**, bring to a boil, and add the hops and other ingredients as specified in the main recipe.

Created by the Moortgat brewery in Belgium at the end of World War I, this style is similar to Tripel (see p157) but paler, less malty, and with a slightly bitter finish.

Belgian Strong Golden Ale

ORIGINAL GRAVITY 1072 **EXPECTED FINAL GRAVITY** 1012 **TOTAL LIQUOR** 33 LITRES (58 PINTS)

 MAKES
23 LITRES
(40 PINTS)

 READY TO DRINK
8 WEEKS

 ESTIMATED ABV
7.9%

 BITTERNESS RATING
30 IBU

 COLOUR RATING
10 EBC

FOR THE MASH

LIQUOR 15 litres (26 pints) **MASH TIME** 1 hr **TEMPERATURE** 65°C (149°F)

Grain bill	Quantity
Belgian Pilsner malt	5.6kg (12lb 6oz)
Carapils malt	450g (1lb)
Aromatic malt	300g (10½oz)

FOR THE BOIL

LIQUOR 27 litres (47½ pints) **BOIL TIME** 1 hr 10 mins

Hops	Quantity	IBU	When to add
Saaz 4.2%	47g (1⅔oz)	18.6	At start of boil
Tettnang 4.5%	58g (2oz)	11.7	For last 15 mins of boil

Other			
Protofloc	1 tsp		For last 15 mins of boil
Belgian light candi crystals	750g (1lb 10oz)		For last 5 mins of boil

TO FERMENT

FERMENTATION 24°C (75°F) **CONDITIONING** 7 weeks at 12°C (54°F)

Yeast
Wyeast 1762 Belgian Abbey II

MALT EXTRACT VERSION

Steep 450g (1lb) **Carapils malt** in 27 litres (47½ pints) of water at 65°C (149°F) for 30 mins. Remove the malt, then add 3.6kg (8lb) **dried extra light malt extract**, bring to a boil, and add the hops as specified in the main recipe.

Stronger, paler, and less sweet than its southern counterpart, Northern Brown Ale has a nutty, chocolaty character with a moderately hoppy finish.

Northern Brown Ale

ORIGINAL GRAVITY 1052 EXPECTED FINAL GRAVITY 1013 TOTAL LIQUOR 32.5 LITRES (57 PINTS)

 MAKES 23 LITRES (40 PINTS)

 READY TO DRINK 6 WEEKS

 ESTIMATED ABV 5.1 %

 BITTERNESS RATING 25.7 IBU

 COLOUR RATING 27.2 EBC

FOR THE MASH

LIQUOR 13 litres (23 pints) MASH TIME 1 hr TEMPERATURE 65°C (149°F)

Grain bill	Quantity
Pale malt	4.8kg (10lb 9oz)
Crystal malt	250g (9oz)
Chocolate malt	100g (3½oz)

FOR THE BOIL

LIQUOR 27 litres (47½ pints) BOIL TIME 1 hr 10 mins

Hops	Quantity	IBU	When to add
Admiral 14.5%	16g (½oz)	25.7	At start of boil
Challenger 7%	16g (½oz)	0.0	At turn off

Other			
Protofloc	1 tsp		For last 15 mins of boil

TO FERMENT

FERMENTATION 20°C (68°F)
CONDITIONING 5 weeks at 12°C (54°F)

Yeast
Wyeast 1098 English ale

MALT EXTRACT VERSION

Steep 250g (9oz) **crystal malt** and 100g (3½oz) **chocolate malt** in 27 litres (47½ pints) of water at 65°C (149°F) for 30 mins. Remove the malt, then add 3.3kg (7lb 4oz) **dried light malt extract**, bring to a boil, and add the hops as specified in the main recipe.

Also known as London ale, this style originated in the early 20th century as an alternative to porter and mild. Moderately low in alcohol, it has a sweet, malty finish.

QUICK BREW

Southern Brown Ale

ORIGINAL GRAVITY 1041 **EXPECTED FINAL GRAVITY** 1012 **TOTAL LIQUOR** 31 LITRES (54½ PINTS)

 MAKES 23 LITRES (40 PINTS)

 READY TO DRINK 4 WEEKS

 ESTIMATED ABV 3.8%

 **BITTERNESS RATING** 17.4 IBU

 COLOUR RATING 37.6 EBC

FOR THE MASH

LIQUOR 10 litres (17½ pints) **MASH TIME** 1 hr **TEMPERATURE** 65°C (149°F)

Grain bill	Quantity
Pale malt	3.5kg (7lb 11oz)
Dark crystal malt	300g (10½oz)
Chocolate malt	110g (4oz)
Torrified wheat	100g (3½oz)
Black malt	55g (2oz)

FOR THE BOIL

LIQUOR 27 litres (47½ pints) **BOIL TIME** 1 hr 10 mins

Hops	Quantity	IBU	When to add
Fuggle 4.5%	24g (¾oz)	12.9	At start of boil
Fuggle 4.5%	24g (¾oz)	4.5	For last 10 mins of boil

Other			
Protofloc	1 tsp		For last 15 mins of boil

TO FERMENT

FERMENTATION 22°C (72°F) **CONDITIONING** 3 weeks at 12°C (54°F)

Yeast
Wyeast 1187 Ringwood ale

MALT EXTRACT VERSION

Steep 300g (10½oz) **dark crystal malt**, 110g (4oz) **chocolate malt**, and 55g (2oz) **black malt** in 27 litres (47½ pints) of water at 65°C (149°F) for 30 mins. Remove the malt, then add 2.3kg (5lb 1oz) **dried light malt extract**, bring to a boil, and add the hops as specified in the main recipe.

BREWER'S TIP
If you would prefer a slightly drier-tasting beer, try using Wyeast 1099 Whitbread ale instead of the Ringwood.

Dark and strong with fruity, sherry-like flavours from the corn sugar, this special beer requires a long conditioning period to fully develop its character.

Old Ale

ORIGINAL GRAVITY 1079 **EXPECTED FINAL GRAVITY** 1014 **TOTAL LIQUOR** 34 LITRES (60 PINTS)

 MAKES
23 LITRES (40 PINTS)

 **READY TO DRINK**
12 WEEKS

 ESTIMATED ABV
8.7%

 BITTERNESS RATING
55 IBU

 COLOUR RATING
32.6 EBC

FOR THE MASH

LIQUOR 16.75 litres (29½ pints) **MASH TIME** 1 hr **TEMPERATURE** 68°C (154°F)

Grain bill	Quantity
Pale malt	4.5kg (10lb)
Munich malt	1.8kg (4lb)
Dark crystal malt	300g (10½oz)
Chocolate malt	100g (3½oz)

FOR THE BOIL

LIQUOR 27 litres (47½ pints) **BOIL TIME** 1 hr 10 mins

Hops	Quantity	IBU	When to add
Golding 5.5%	76g (2¾oz)	37.3	At start of boil
Golding 5.5%	76g (2¾oz)	13.1	For last 10 mins of boil

Other			
Protofloc	1 tsp		For last 15 mins of boil
Corn sugar	650g (1lb 7oz)		For last 5 mins of boil

TO FERMENT

FERMENTATION 20°C (68°F) **CONDITIONING** 11 weeks at 12°C (54°F)

Yeast
Wyeast 1028 English ale

BREWER'S TIP

To give your beer a festive twist, try adding some Christmas spices to the fermenter. Cinnamon, nutmeg, and cloves will all work well.

A traditional British-style Mild, this dark ale is moderately low in alcohol with fruity, chocolaty, malt flavours and a dry, hoppy finish.

QUICK BREW

Mild

ORIGINAL GRAVITY 1036   EXPECTED FINAL GRAVITY 1011   TOTAL LIQUOR 30 LITRES (53 PINTS)

MAKES
23 LITRES
(40 PINTS)

READY TO DRINK
4 WEEKS

ESTIMATED ABV
3.3%

BITTERNESS RATING
21.2 IBU

COLOUR RATING
33.5 EBC

FOR THE MASH

LIQUOR 9 litres (16 pints)   MASH TIME 1 hr   TEMPERATURE 68°C (154°F)

Grain bill	Quantity
Mild ale malt	3kg (6lb 10oz)
Dark crystal malt	500g (1lb 2oz)
Chocolate malt	100g (3½oz)

FOR THE BOIL

LIQUOR 27 litres (47½ pints)   BOIL TIME 1 hr 10 mins

Hops	Quantity	IBU	When to add
Northdown 8%	20g (⅔oz)	19.7	At start of boil
Bramling Cross 6%	10g (⅓oz)	0.0	For last 5 mins of boil

Other			
Protofloc	1 tsp		For last 15 mins of boil

TO FERMENT

FERMENTATION 20°C (68°F)
CONDITIONING 3 weeks at 12°C (54°F)

Yeast
Wyeast 1318 London ale III

MALT EXTRACT VERSION

Steep 500g (1lb 2oz) **dark crystal malt** and 100g (3½oz) **chocolate malt** in 27 litres (47½ pints) of water at 65°C (149°F) for 30 mins. Remove the malt, then add 1.9kg (4lb 3oz) **dried light malt extract**, bring to a boil, and add the hops as specified in the main recipe.

This dark, strong ale has delicious malty and chocolaty flavours balanced by a light, hoppy bitterness. Ruby Mild is perfect served with steak and chips.

Ruby Mild

ORIGINAL GRAVITY 1049 **EXPECTED FINAL GRAVITY** 1014 **TOTAL LIQUOR** 32 LITRES (56 PINTS)

MAKES 23 LITRES (40 PINTS)	**READY TO DRINK** 8 WEEKS	**ESTIMATED ABV** 4.6%	**BITTERNESS RATING** 18.1 IBU	**COLOUR RATING** 31.6 EBC

FOR THE MASH

LIQUOR 12.3 litres (21½ pints) **MASH TIME** 1 hr **TEMPERATURE** 66°C (150°F)

Grain bill	Quantity
Pale malt	4.5kg (10lb)
Crystal malt	150g (5½oz)
Chocolate malt	150g (5½oz)
Torrified wheat malt	125g (4½oz)

FOR THE BOIL

LIQUOR 27 litres (47½ pints) **BOIL TIME** 1 hr 10 mins

Hops	Quantity	IBU	When to add
Golding 5.5%	30g (1oz)	18.1	At start of boil
Golding 5.5%	15g (½oz)	0.0	At turn off
Other			
Protofloc	1 tsp		For last 15 mins of boil

TO FERMENT

FERMENTATION 22°C (72°F) **CONDITIONING** at least 4 weeks at 12°C (54°F)

Yeast
Wyeast 1187 Ringwood ale

Withdrawn from Stock

MALT EXTRACT VERSION

Steep 150g (5½oz) **crystal malt** and 150g (5½oz) **chocolate malt** in 27 litres (47½ pints) of water at 65°C (149°F) for 30 mins. Remove the malt, then add 2.9kg (6lb 6oz) **dried light malt extract**, bring to a boil, and add the hops as specified in the main recipe.

One of the strongest beers produced by any brewery, English Barley Wine has a complex, malty, sherry-like flavour with a lingering hoppy bitterness on the finish.

English Barley Wine

ORIGINAL GRAVITY 1090 **EXPECTED FINAL GRAVITY** 1019 **TOTAL LIQUOR** 35.5 LITRES (62½ PINTS)

 MAKES 23 LITRES (40 PINTS)

 READY TO DRINK 15 WEEKS

 ESTIMATED ABV 9.6%

 BITTERNESS RATING 50 IBU

 COLOUR RATING 27.3 EBC

FOR THE MASH

LIQUOR 21 litres (37 pints) **MASH TIME** 1 hr **TEMPERATURE** 67°C (153°F)

Grain bill	Quantity
Pale malt	7.2kg (16lb)
Dark crystal malt	300g (10½oz)
Carapils malt	800g (1¾lb)

FOR THE BOIL

LIQUOR 27 litres (47½ pints) **BOIL TIME** 1 hr 30 mins

Hops	Quantity	IBU	When to add
Northdown 8%	71g (2½oz)	50.0	At start of boil
East Kent Golding 5.5%	14g (½oz)	0.0	At turn off
Target 10.5%	14g (½oz)	0.0	At turn off

Other			
Protofloc	1 tsp		For last 15 mins of boil
Honey	500g (1lb 2oz)		For last 5 mins of boil

TO FERMENT

FERMENTATION 22°C (72°F) **CONDITIONING** 14 weeks at 12°C (54°F)

Yeast
Wyeast 1028 English ale

MALT EXTRACT VERSION

Steep 300g (10½oz) **dark crystal malt** and 800g (1¾lb) **Carapils malt** in 27 litres (47½ pints) of water at 65°C (149°F) for 30 mins. Remove the malt, then add 4.5kg (10lb) **dried light malt extract**, bring to a boil, and add the hops as specified in the main recipe.

BREWER'S TIP
If your mash tun isn't large enough for all the malts in the grain bill, reduce the pale malt to 5kg (11lb) and add 1.3kg (2lb 14oz) dried malt extract to the boil.

Far hoppier than its English counterpart, American Barley Wine is a strong and intense style of beer with a bittersweet aftertaste and robust citrus aroma.

American Barley Wine

ORIGINAL GRAVITY 1105   EXPECTED FINAL GRAVITY 1024   TOTAL LIQUOR 37.5 LITRES (66 PINTS)

 MAKES 23 LITRES (40 PINTS)   **READY TO DRINK** 15 WEEKS   **ESTIMATED ABV** 10.9%   **BITTERNESS RATING** 66 IBU   **COLOUR RATING** 25.4 EBC

FOR THE MASH

LIQUOR 26 litres (46 pints)   **MASH TIME** 1 hr   **TEMPERATURE** 67°C (153°F)

Grain bill	Quantity
Pale malt	10kg (22lb 1oz)
Crystal malt	400g (14oz)
Carafa special III malt	30g (1oz)

FOR THE BOIL

LIQUOR 27 litres (47½ pints)   **BOIL TIME** 1 hr 10 mins

Hops	Quantity	IBU	When to add
Chinook 13.3%	71g (2½oz)	61.7	At start of boil
Cascade 6.6%	26g (1oz)	4.3	For last 10 mins of boil
Cascade 6.6%	100g (3½oz)	0.0	At turn off

Other			
Protofloc	1 tsp		For last 15 mins of boil

TO FERMENT

FERMENTATION 4 days at 18°C (64°F), then 22°C (72°F) until completion
CONDITIONING 13 weeks at 12°C (54°F)

Yeast
Wyeast 1056 American ale

MALT EXTRACT VERSION

Steep 400g (14oz) **crystal malt** and 30g (1oz) **Carafa special III malt** in 27 litres (47½ pints) of water at 65°C (149°F) for 30 mins. Remove the malt, then add 6.3kg (14lb) **dried light malt extract**, bring to a boil, and add the hops as specified in the main recipe.

BREWER'S TIP

This is a strong beer to enjoy in moderation, so consider halving the weights and volumes given in the recipe to brew a half batch.

A soft, sweet beer with lovely caramel flavours, this brew has more substance and roast flavours than a brown ale, and has a delicious chocolate aftertaste.

Brown Porter

ORIGINAL GRAVITY 1049 **EXPECTED FINAL GRAVITY** 1012 **TOTAL LIQUOR** 32 LITRES (56 PINTS)

 MAKES 23 LITRES (40 PINTS)
 READY TO DRINK 5 WEEKS
 ESTIMATED ABV 4.9%
 BITTERNESS RATING 30.2 IBU
 COLOUR RATING 45 EBC

FOR THE MASH

LIQUOR 12.5 litres (22 pints) **MASH TIME** 1 hr **TEMPERATURE** 67°C (153°F)

Grain bill	Quantity
Pale malt	4kg (8lb 13oz)
Dark crystal malt	350g (12oz)
Chocolate malt	200g (7oz)
Brown malt	300g (10½oz)

FOR THE BOIL

LIQUOR 27 litres (47½ pints) **BOIL TIME** 1 hr 10 mins

Hops	Quantity	IBU	When to add
First Gold 8.0%	31g (1oz)	27.6	At start of boil
First Gold 8.0%	15g (½oz)	2.7	For last 10 mins of boil

Other			
Protofloc	1 tsp		For last 15 mins of boil

TO FERMENT

FERMENTATION 18°C (64°F) **CONDITIONING** 4 weeks at 12°C (54°F)

Yeast
Wyeast 1028 London ale

MALT EXTRACT VERSION

Steep 350g (12oz) **dark crystal malt**, 200g (7oz) **chocolate malt**, and 300g (10½oz) **brown malt** in 27 litres (47½ pints) of water at 65°C (149°F) for 30 mins. Remove the malt, then add 2.5kg (5½lb) **dried light malt extract**, bring to a boil, and add the hops as specified in the main recipe.

Rich and smoky malt flavours combine perfectly with subtle red-berry flavours to create this irresistible, dark, reddish-brown winter ale.

Smoked Porter

ORIGINAL GRAVITY 1054 **EXPECTED FINAL GRAVITY** 1016 **TOTAL LIQUOR** 33 LITRES (58 PINTS)

 MAKES
23 LITRES
(40 PINTS)

 READY TO DRINK
6 WEEKS

 ESTIMATED ABV
5.1%

 BITTERNESS RATING
28 IBU

 COLOUR RATING
49.6 EBC

FOR THE MASH

LIQUOR 14.75 litres (26 pints) **MASH TIME** 1 hr **TEMPERATURE** 65°C (149°F)

Grain bill	Quantity
Pale malt	4.5kg (10lb)
Smoked malt	700g (1lb 8oz)
Black malt	300g (10½oz)
Crystal malt	200g (7oz)
Caramunich I malt	200g (7oz)

FOR THE BOIL

LIQUOR 27 litres (47½ pints) **BOIL TIME** 1 hr 15 mins

Hops	Quantity	IBU	When to add
Challenger 7%	35g (1¼oz)	23.8	At start of boil
Willamette 6.3%	20g (⅔oz)	4.2	For last 10 mins of boil
Willamette 6.3%	20g (⅔oz)	0.0	At turn off
Other			
Protofloc	1 tsp		For last 15 mins of boil

TO FERMENT

FERMENTATION 18°C (64°F) **CONDITIONING** 5 weeks at 12°C (54°F)

Yeast
Wyeast 1187 Ringwood ale

BREWER'S TIP

For heightened smokiness, try adding 100g (3½oz) toasted oak chips to the fermenter after 4 days.

A strong, warming beer with complex fruit flavours and a smooth, clean finish. As the name suggests, this porter originates from countries bordering the Baltic Sea.

Baltic Porter

ORIGINAL GRAVITY 1080   **EXPECTED FINAL GRAVITY** 1019   **TOTAL LIQUOR** 35 LITRES (61½ PINTS)

 **MAKES**
23 LITRES
(40 PINTS)

 READY TO DRINK
12+ WEEKS

 ESTIMATED ABV
8.2%

 BITTERNESS RATING
30.2 IBU

 COLOUR RATING
56.3 EBC

FOR THE MASH

LIQUOR 19.2 litres (33¾ pints)   **MASH TIME** 1 hr   **TEMPERATURE** 67°C (153°F)

Grain bill	Quantity
Munich malt	7kg (15lb 5oz)
Amber malt	300g (10½oz)
Carafa special III	286g (10oz)
Biscuit malt	200g (7oz)
Chocolate malt	300g (10½oz)
Caramunich I malt	100g (3½oz)

FOR THE BOIL

LIQUOR 27 litres (47½ pints)   **BOIL TIME** 1 hr 10 mins

Hops	Quantity	IBU	When to add
Saaz 4.2%	74g (2½oz)	27.4	At start of boil
Saaz 4.2%	15g (½oz)	2.6	For last 15 mins of boil

Other			
Protofloc	1 tsp		For last 15 mins of boil

TO FERMENT

FERMENTATION 12°C (54°F)   **CONDITIONING** 11+ weeks at 12°C (54°F)

Yeast
Wyeast 2633 Oktoberfest lager blend

BREWER'S TIP
This beer will continue to age extremely well, so bottle it and leave for as long as possible for a superior quality brew.

This is a dark, complex, and full-bodied ale with a dry finish. It is similar in style to Brown Porter (see p169) but has a unique character thanks to the addition of honey.

Honey Porter

ORIGINAL GRAVITY 1048 **EXPECTED FINAL GRAVITY** 1009 **TOTAL LIQUOR** 32 LITRES (56 PINTS)

 MAKES 23 LITRES (40 PINTS)   **READY TO DRINK** 6 WEEKS   **ESTIMATED ABV** 5.2%   **BITTERNESS RATING** 19.8 IBU   **COLOUR RATING** 50.3 EBC

FOR THE MASH

LIQUOR 10.5 litres (18½ pints) **MASH TIME** 1 hr **TEMPERATURE** 65°C (149°F)

Grain bill	Quantity
Pale malt	3kg (6lb 10oz)
Light crystal malt	500g (1lb 2oz)
Vienna malt	400g (14oz)
Carafa special III	200g (7oz)
Chocolate malt	100g (3½oz)

FOR THE BOIL

LIQUOR 27 litres (47½ pints) **BOIL TIME** 1 hr 10 mins

Hops	Quantity	IBU	When to add
Fuggle 4.5%	23g (¾oz)	10.8	At start of boil
Challenger 7%	15g (½oz)	4.3	For last 10 mins of boil
Wakatu 6.6%	16g (½oz)	0.0	At turn off
Other			
Protofloc	1 tsp		For last 15 mins of boil
Honey	500g (1lb 2oz)		For last 5 mins of boil

TO FERMENT

FERMENTATION 18°C (64°F) **CONDITIONING** 5 weeks at 12°C (54°F)

Yeast
Wyeast 1272 American ale II

This Irish stout was first created to emulate the success of London-style porters. Creamier and more full-bodied than a porter, however, this is a classic, rich-flavoured stout.

Dry Stout

ORIGINAL GRAVITY 1048 **EXPECTED FINAL GRAVITY** 1013 **TOTAL LIQUOR** 32 LITRES (56 PINTS)

 MAKES 23 LITRES (40 PINTS)

 READY TO DRINK 5 WEEKS

 ESTIMATED ABV 4.7%

 BITTERNESS RATING 37.9 IBU

 COLOUR RATING 76.7 EBC

FOR THE MASH

LIQUOR 12 litres (21 pints) **MASH TIME** 1 hr **TEMPERATURE** 67°C (153°F)

Grain bill	Quantity
Pale malt	3.8kg (8lb 6oz)
Flaked barley	500g (1lb 2oz)
Roasted barley	450g (1lb)
Chocolate malt	100g (3½oz)

FOR THE BOIL

LIQUOR 27 litres (47½ pints) **BOIL TIME** 1 hr 10 mins

Hops	Quantity	IBU	When to add
East Kent Golding 5.5%	61g (2oz)	37.9	At start of boil
Other			
Protofloc	1 tsp		For last 15 mins of boil

TO FERMENT

FERMENTATION 18°C (64°F)
CONDITIONING 4 weeks at 12°C (54°F)

Yeast
Wyeast 1084 Irish ale

With an irresistibly smooth texture and rich, roasted chocolate flavours, Oatmeal Stout is a delicious, comforting beer to be enjoyed in the winter months.

Oatmeal Stout

ORIGINAL GRAVITY 1049 **EXPECTED FINAL GRAVITY** 1014 **TOTAL LIQUOR** 32 LITRES (56 PINTS)

 MAKES 23 LITRES (40 PINTS)

 READY TO DRINK 5 WEEKS

 ESTIMATED ABV 4.6%

 BITTERNESS RATING 30.3 IBU

COLOUR RATING 43.9 EBC

FOR THE MASH

LIQUOR 12.2 litres (21½ pints) **MASH TIME** 1 hr **TEMPERATURE** 67°C (153°F)

Grain bill	Quantity
Pale malt	4.2kg (9lb 2oz)
Rolled oats	250g (9oz)
Crystal malt	200g (7oz)
Chocolate malt	160g (5⅔oz)
Roasted barley	70g (2½oz)

FOR THE BOIL

LIQUOR 27 litres (47½ pints) **BOIL TIME** 1 hr 10 mins

Hops	Quantity	IBU	When to add
Challenger 7%	39g (1½oz)	30.3	At start of boil
Challenger 7%	16g (½oz)	0.0	At turn off
Golding 5.5%	16g (½oz)	0.0	At turn off
Other			
Protofloc	1 tsp		For last 15 mins of boil

TO FERMENT

FERMENTATION 20°C (68°F) **CONDITIONING** 4 weeks at 12°C (54°F)

Yeast
Wyeast 1187 Ringwood ale

BREWER'S TIP

Be careful not to introduce extra oxygen (eg, from splashing) while bottling this beer – the addition of oats makes it susceptible to going stale.

Chocolate and rich, roasted coffee flavours complement the light citrus hop aromas in this American-style stout. Use freshly ground coffee for the best results.

Coffee Stout

ORIGINAL GRAVITY 1058 **EXPECTED FINAL GRAVITY** 1015 **TOTAL LIQUOR** 33 LITRES (58 PINTS)

 MAKES 23 LITRES (40 PINTS)   **READY TO DRINK** 6 WEEKS   **ESTIMATED ABV** 5.7%   **BITTERNESS RATING** 40.6 IBU   **COLOUR RATING** 79.2 EBC

FOR THE MASH

LIQUOR 14.6 litres (25⅔ pints) **MASH TIME** 1 hr **TEMPERATURE** 67°C (153°F)

Grain bill	Quantity
Pale malt	5kg (11lb)
Roasted barley malt	250g (9oz)
Carafa special I malt	250g (9oz)
Light crystal malt	200g (7oz)
Caramunich I malt	200g (7oz)
Chocolate malt	150g (5½oz)

FOR THE BOIL

LIQUOR 27 litres (47½ pints) **BOIL TIME** 1 hr 15 mins

Hops	Quantity	IBU	When to add
Magnum 16%	21g (¾oz)	35.5	At start of boil
Cascade 6.6%	21g (¾oz)	5.5	For last 10 mins of boil
Cascade 6.6%	21g (¾oz)	0.0	At turn off

Other			
Protofloc	1 tsp		For last 15 mins of boil

TO FERMENT

FERMENTATION 18°C (64°F) **CONDITIONING** 5 weeks at 12°C (54°F)

Yeast
Wyeast 1084 Irish ale

Other	Quantity	When to add
Fresh coffee	500ml (16fl oz)	After 4 days

Heavy citrus aromas and flavours perfectly complement the dark, bitter, roasted malt flavours in this American twist on traditional English and Irish stouts.

American Stout

ORIGINAL GRAVITY 1060 **EXPECTED FINAL GRAVITY** 1010 **TOTAL LIQUOR** 33 LITRES (58 PINTS)

 MAKES 23 LITRES (40 PINTS)   **READY TO DRINK** 8 WEEKS   **ESTIMATED ABV** 6.2%   **BITTERNESS RATING** 39.9 IBU   **COLOUR RATING** 76.7 EBC

FOR THE MASH
LIQUOR 15 litres (26 pints) **MASH TIME** 1 hr **TEMPERATURE** 65°C (149°F)

Grain bill	Quantity
Pale malt	3kg (6lb 10oz)
Munich malt	2kg (4½lb)
Black malt	500g (1lb 2oz)
Crystal malt	500g (1lb 2oz)

FOR THE BOIL
LIQUOR 27 litres (47½ pints) **BOIL TIME** 1 hr 15 mins

Hops	Quantity	IBU	When to add
Chinook 13.3%	28g (1oz)	38.1	At start of boil
Amarillo 5%	10g (⅓oz)	1.8	For last 10 mins of boil
Amarillo 5%	50g (1¾oz)	0.0	At turn off

Other			
Protofloc	1 tsp		For last 15 mins of boil

TO FERMENT
FERMENTATION 18°C (64°F) **CONDITIONING** 7 weeks at 12°C (54°F)

Yeast
Whitelabs WLP001 California ale

Milk Stout was traditionally made by adding milk to porter – for serving to labourers at lunchtime. It is a silky smooth beer with hints of chocolate and coffee.

Milk Stout

ORIGINAL GRAVITY 1059 **EXPECTED FINAL GRAVITY** 1018 **TOTAL LIQUOR** 32.5 LITRES (57 PINTS)

 MAKES 23 LITRES (40 PINTS)
 READY TO DRINK 5 WEEKS
 ESTIMATED ABV 5.2%
 BITTERNESS RATING 25 IBU
 COLOUR RATING 63.6 EBC

FOR THE MASH

LIQUOR 13.5 litres (23¾ pints) **MASH TIME** 1 hr **TEMPERATURE** 67°C (153°F)

Grain bill	Quantity
Pale malt	4.2kg (9lb 2oz)
Chocolate malt	300g (10½oz)
Crystal malt	300g (10½oz)
Roasted barley	200g (7oz)
Flaked barley	200g (7oz)
Special B malt	200g (7oz)

FOR THE BOIL

LIQUOR 27 litres (47½ pints) **BOIL TIME** 1 hr 15 mins

Hops	Quantity	IBU	When to add
Challenger 7%	29g (1oz)	21.7	At start of boil
Golding 5.5%	11g (⅓oz)	3.3	For last 15 mins of boil

Other			
Protofloc	1 tsp		For last 15 mins of boil
Lactose sugar	300g (10½oz)		For last 10 mins of boil

TO FERMENT

FERMENTATION 20°C (68°F) **CONDITIONING** 4 weeks at 12°C (54°F)

Yeast
Wyeast 1318 London ale III

BREWER'S TIP

The lactose sugar is a non-fermentable sugar, so increase the quantity if you prefer a sweeter beer.

Originally brewed in England for export to the courts of the Russian Tsars, the high alcohol and hopping rates in this beer preserved it and prevented it from freezing.

Russian Imperial Stout

ORIGINAL GRAVITY 1080 **EXPECTED FINAL GRAVITY** 1019 **TOTAL LIQUOR** 35 LITRES (61½ PINTS)

 MAKES 23 LITRES (40 PINTS)

 READY TO DRINK 16 WEEKS

 ESTIMATED ABV 8.2%

 BITTERNESS RATING 60 IBU

 COLOUR RATING 76.3 EBC

FOR THE MASH

LIQUOR 20 litres (35 pints) **MASH TIME** 1 hr **TEMPERATURE** 65°C (149°F)

Grain bill	Quantity
Pale malt	7kg (15lb 5oz)
Crystal malt	500g (1lb 2oz)
Roasted barley	200g (7oz)
Chocolate malt	150g (5½oz)
Carafa special III malt	150g (5½oz)

FOR THE BOIL

LIQUOR 27 litres (47½ pints) **BOIL TIME** 1 hr 15 mins

Hops	Quantity	IBU	When to add
Challenger 7%	61g (2oz)	37.9	At start of boil
Golding 5.5%	61g (2oz)	22.2	For last 30 mins of boil

Other			
Protofloc	1 tsp		For last 15 mins of boil

TO FERMENT

FERMENTATION 20°C (68°F) **CONDITIONING** 15 weeks at 12°C (54°F)

Yeast
Wyeast 1028 London ale

MALT EXTRACT VERSION

Steep 500g (1lb 2oz) **crystal malt**, 200g (7oz) **roasted barley**, 150g (5½oz) **chocolate malt**, and 150g (5½oz) **Carafa special III malt** in 27 litres (47½ pints) of water at 65°C (149°F) for 30 mins. Remove the malt, then add 4.4kg (9lb 11oz) **dried light malt extract**, bring to a boil, and add the hops as specified in the main recipe.

This delicious beer combines a dark, rich maltiness, subtle vanilla aroma, and sweet bourbon finish. Brew well in advance and leave to mature for several months.

Vanilla Bourbon Stout

ORIGINAL GRAVITY 1070 **EXPECTED FINAL GRAVITY** 1017 **TOTAL LIQUOR** 34 LITRES (60 PINTS)

 MAKES 23 LITRES (40 PINTS)   **READY TO DRINK** 16 WEEKS   **ESTIMATED ABV** 7.8%   **BITTERNESS RATING** 30.2 IBU   **COLOUR RATING** 58.6 EBC

FOR THE MASH

LIQUOR 17.5 litres (30¾ pints) **MASH TIME** 1 hr **TEMPERATURE** 65°C (149°F)

Grain bill	Quantity
Pale malt	4.9kg (10lb 13oz)
Vienna malt	1.1kg (2½lb)
Brown malt	500g (1lb 2oz)
Chocolate malt	350g (12oz)
Crystal malt	200g (7oz)

FOR THE BOIL

LIQUOR 27 litres (47½ pints) **BOIL TIME** 1 hr 15 mins

Hops	Quantity	IBU	When to add
Northern Brewer 8%	35g (1¼oz)	26.6	At start of boil
Challenger 7%	16g (½oz)	3.6	For last 10 mins of boil

Other			
Protofloc	1 tsp		For last 15 mins of boil

TO FERMENT

FERMENTATION 20°C (68°F) **CONDITIONING** 15 weeks at 12°C (54°F)

Yeast
Wyeast 1028 London ale

Other	Quantity	When to add
Vanilla pods	2 pods	Dry hop after 4 days, leave for about 1 week
Bourbon	400ml	Just before bottling

Wheat beers

Widely brewed in Medieval Europe, wheat beers – also known as white beers – are produced with a large ratio of wheat in the mash tun.

Wheat often makes up more than 50 per cent of the grain bill in this style, and is typically mixed with pale malt. This results in a hazy beer with a distinctly dry character – although most of the flavours are produced from the special strains of yeast that are used.

TOP-CROPPING YEAST

Wheat-style yeasts are true top-cropping yeasts, meaning they produce an exceptionally large head during fermentation as all the yeast rises to the top of the wort. The higher fermentation temperatures result in complex flavour compounds and esters being produced, which would normally be viewed as a fault in other beer styles. Clove, spice, banana, and sometimes bubble-gum characters can all be found in these delightful beers. Belgian wheat beers, for example, often have a particularly distinct character from the addition of bitter orange peel and spices.

CLOUDY CHARACTER

The unique fermentation and serving technique give this style its particular character. Usually served cool and well carbonated, wheat beers are always conditioned in the bottle. This allows the yeast sediment to be gently roused when serving to produce a cloudy beer.

Wheat beers are easy to recreate at home due to the higher fermentation temperatures and wide range of acceptable flavours. They are also designed to be drunk when young, making them ideal quick brews.

Weissbier

Weissbier (white beer) originates from Bavaria. The name refers to the fact that it was lighter in colour than other ales from the region.

- **Appearance** Light straw to dark golden, with a thick, long-lasting head. Often served cloudy.

- **Taste** A relatively low bitterness, often with notes of clove, banana, and vanilla.

- **Aroma** Light hop aroma with citrus, banana, and clove characters, without being too overpowering.

- **Strength** 4.3–5.6% ABV

- (DE) There are several styles, mostly from Germany. For example, hefeweizen (yeast wheat) is unfiltered, cloudy, and has a low hop bitterness. Kristallweizen (crystal wheat), on the other hand, is filtered for greater clarity.

See pp184–87

Rye beer

Using rye in the mash adds a grainy flavour. Historically, rye was often used instead of barley in German brewing.

- **Appearance** Light golden to dark, often with a hazy orange or red hue and a dense, long-lasting head.

- **Taste** Grainy with a distinct, spicy rye flavour, similar to that found in pumpernickel or rye bread.

- **Aroma** Light spicy rye aroma, often with clove and banana notes from the fermentation process.

- **Strength** 4.5–6% ABV

- (DE) Wheat yeasts fermented at lower temperatures give a complex banana and clove character to German rye beers.

- (US) American rye beers are strong and highly hopped. Spicy rye flavours are complemented by citrus hops and a fairly neutral yeast character.

See pp188–89

Witbier

A very old, almost lost, style made popular again by Pierre Celis at Hoegaarden. Witbiers are spicy with moderate alcohol levels.

- **Appearance** Very pale straw colours, and always served cloudy with a dense, long-lasting head.

- **Taste** Refreshingly crisp, tart, and spicy with orange fruit characters, and a low hop aroma and bitterness.

- **Aroma** The use of floral hops and spicy coriander gives a distinct, subtle aroma.

- **Strength** 4.5–5.5% ABV

- (BE) Belgian witbiers are generally spiced with coriander, orange, and other spices and herbs.

See pp190–91

Dark wheat beer

A strikingly dark brew with a more complex malt character than other styles of wheat beer.

- **Appearance** Amber to deep brown, with a long-lasting, off-white head; served cloudy and well carbonated.

- **Taste** Banana and clove flavours are present, but tend to be dominated by sweet caramel notes from the roasted malts.

- **Aroma** Moderate clove and banana aromas, with low noble-hop notes.

- **Strength** 4.3–5.6% ABV

- (DE) The German dark wheat style has distinctive banana and clove notes, with caramel malt flavours. It is lightly hopped with European noble hops.

- (US) American dark wheats are stronger and hoppier than German versions. Subtle malt flavours are complemented by citrus hops and a neutral yeast flavour.

See pp192–93

Originally brewed in Munich in 1907, this strong wheat beer is a rich, dark-amber brew with spicy clove-like flavours. It has a long-lasting, light-tan head when served.

QUICK BREW

Weizenbock

ORIGINAL GRAVITY 1065 **EXPECTED FINAL GRAVITY** 1016 **TOTAL LIQUOR** 33.5 LITRES (59 PINTS)

 MAKES 23 LITRES (40 PINTS)

 READY TO DRINK 4 WEEKS

 ESTIMATED ABV 6.6%

 BITTERNESS RATING 19.8 IBU

COLOUR RATING 28.3 EBC

FOR THE MASH

LIQUOR 16 litres (28 pints) **MASH TIME** 1 hr **TEMPERATURE** 65°C (149°F)

Grain bill	Quantity
Wheat malt	3.6kg (8lb)
Munich malt	2.4kg (5lb 5oz)
Carawheat malt	250g (9oz)
Chocolate wheat malt	120g (4¼oz)

FOR THE BOIL

LIQUOR 27 litres (47½ pints) **BOIL TIME** 1 hr 15 mins

Hops	Quantity	IBU	When to add
Saaz 4.2%	48g (1⅔oz)	19.8	At start of boil

Other			
Protofloc	1 tsp		For last 15 mins of boil

TO FERMENT

FERMENTATION 24°C (75°F) **CONDITIONING** 3 weeks at 12°C (54°F)

Yeast
Wyeast 3056 Bavarian wheat

This unique-tasting Bavarian beer is dominated by banana and bubble-gum flavours from the yeast. It is best served cloudy by rousing the yeast sediment when pouring.

QUICK BREW

Weissbier

ORIGINAL GRAVITY 1050 **EXPECTED FINAL GRAVITY** 1012 **TOTAL LIQUOR** 32 LITRES (56 PINTS)

 **MAKES**
23 LITRES
(40 PINTS)

 READY TO DRINK
4 WEEKS

 ESTIMATED ABV
5%

 BITTERNESS RATING
15.3 IBU

 COLOUR RATING
6.3 EBC

FOR THE MASH

LIQUOR 12.5 litres (22 pints) **MASH TIME** 1 hr **TEMPERATURE** 65°C (149°F)

Grain bill	Quantity
Wheat malt	2.7kg (6lb)
Pilsner malt	2.3kg (5lb)

FOR THE BOIL

LIQUOR 27 litres (47½ pints) **BOIL TIME** 1 hr 10 mins

Hops	Quantity	IBU	When to add
Hallertauer Hersbrucker 3.5%	25g (1oz)	9.6	At start of boil
Saaz 4.2%	12g (½oz)	5.7	At start of boil
Other			
Protofloc	1 tsp		For last 15 mins of boil

TO FERMENT

FERMENTATION 22°C (72°F) **CONDITIONING** 3 weeks at 12°C (54°F)

Yeast
Wyeast 3068 Weihenstephan Weizen

MALT EXTRACT VERSION

Add 3kg (6lb 10oz) **dried wheat malt extract** to 27 litres (47½ pints) of water, bring to a boil, and add the hops as specified in the main recipe.

This hazy, refreshing beer is packed with exuberant citrus flavours and aromas, which are imparted by the powerful American hops and yeast.

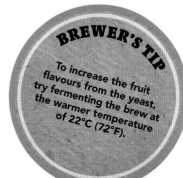

QUICK BREW

American Wheat Beer

ORIGINAL GRAVITY 1058 **EXPECTED FINAL GRAVITY** 1013 **TOTAL LIQUOR** 33 LITRES (58 PINTS)

 MAKES 23 LITRES (40 PINTS)

 READY TO DRINK 4 WEEKS

 ESTIMATED ABV 5.9%

 BITTERNESS RATING 25 IBU

 COLOUR RATING 9.1 EBC

FOR THE MASH

LIQUOR 14.5 litres (25½ pints) **MASH TIME** 1 hr **TEMPERATURE** 65°C (149°F)

Grain bill	Quantity
Wheat malt	3kg (6lb 10oz)
Lager malt	2.5kg (5½lb)
Carapils malt	300g (10½oz)

FOR THE BOIL

LIQUOR 27 litres (47½ pints) **BOIL TIME** 1 hr 10 mins

Hops	Quantity	IBU	When to add
Citra 13.8%	17g (⅔oz)	25.0	At start of boil
Citra 13.8%	26g (1oz)	0.0	At turn off
Other			
Protofloc	1 tsp		For last 15 mins of boil

TO FERMENT

FERMENTATION 18°C (64°F) **CONDITIONING** 3 weeks at 12°C (54°F)

Yeast
Wyeast 1010 American wheat

MALT EXTRACT VERSION

Steep 300g (10½oz) **Carapils malt** in 27 litres (47½ pints) of water at 65°C (149°F) for 30 mins. Remove the malt, then add 3.3kg (7lb 4oz) **dried wheat malt extract**, bring to a boil, and add the hops as specified in the main recipe.

BREWER'S TIP
To increase the fruit flavours from the yeast, try fermenting the brew at the warmer temperature of 22°C (72°F).

Originating from Bavaria, this unusual beer combines a strong, spicy flavour from the rye malt with complex apple, pear, and banana notes from the yeast.

QUICK BREW

Roggenbier

ORIGINAL GRAVITY 1051 **EXPECTED FINAL GRAVITY** 1013 **TOTAL LIQUOR** 32 LITRES (56 PINTS)

 MAKES
23 LITRES
(40 PINTS)

 READY TO DRINK
4 WEEKS

 ESTIMATED ABV
5%

 BITTERNESS RATING
14.6 IBU

 COLOUR RATING
30.9 EBC

FOR THE MASH

LIQUOR 12.25 litres (21½ pints) **MASH TIME** 1 hr **TEMPERATURE** 65°C (149°F)

Grain bill	Quantity
Rye malt	2.9kg (6lb 6oz)
Munich malt	1.6kg (3lb 8oz)
Crystal wheat malt	300g (10½oz)
Carafa special III	120g (4¼oz)

FOR THE BOIL

LIQUOR 27 litres (47½ pints) **BOIL TIME** 1 hr 15 mins

Hops	Quantity	IBU	When to add
Hallertauer Hersbrucker 3.5%	31g (1oz)	11.7	At start of boil
Hallertauer Hersbrucker 3.5%	15g (½oz)	2.8	For last 10 mins of boil
Tettnang 4.5%	15g (½oz)	0.0	At turn off
Other			
Protofloc	1 tsp		For last 15 mins of boil

TO FERMENT

FERMENTATION 24°C (75°F) **CONDITIONING** 3 weeks at 12°C (54°F)

Yeast
Wyeast 3338 Bavarian wheat

Roggenbier

Light, crisp, and slightly spicy, this beer has refreshing citrus notes from the American hops, which are complemented by a clean finish from the German yeast.

QUICK BREW

Rye Beer

ORIGINAL GRAVITY 1056 **EXPECTED FINAL GRAVITY** 1013 **TOTAL LIQUOR** 32.5 LITRES (57 PINTS)

 MAKES 23 LITRES (40 PINTS)   **READY TO DRINK** 4 WEEKS   **ESTIMATED ABV** 5.6%   **BITTERNESS RATING** 25.5 IBU   **COLOUR RATING** 9.8 EBC

FOR THE MASH
LIQUOR 13.75 litres (24¼ pints) **MASH TIME** 1 hr **TEMPERATURE** 65°C (149°F)

Grain bill	Quantity
Rye malt	3kg (6lb 10oz)
Pale malt	2.5kg (5½lb)

FOR THE BOIL
LIQUOR 27 litres (47½ pints) **BOIL TIME** 1 hr 10 mins

Hops	Quantity	IBU	When to add
Chinook 13.3%	18g (⅔oz)	25.5	At start of boil
Amarillo 5%	50g (1¾oz)	0.0	At turn off

Other		
Protofloc	1 tsp	For last 15 mins of boil

TO FERMENT
FERMENTATION 18°C (64°F) **CONDITIONING** 3 weeks at 12°C (54°F)

Yeast
Wyeast 2565 Kölsch

Hops	Quantity	When to add
Amarillo 5%	25g (1oz)	After 4 days, leave for about 1 week

This is a classic, Belgian-style cloudy beer. A spicy coriander flavour mixes with complex banana and orange notes to give this "white beer" its distinct character.

Witbier

ORIGINAL GRAVITY 1045 EXPECTED FINAL GRAVITY 1011 TOTAL LIQUOR 31.5 LITRES (55½ PINTS)

 MAKES
23 LITRES
(40 PINTS)

 READY TO DRINK
4 WEEKS

 ESTIMATED ABV
4.5%

 BITTERNESS RATING
15.3 IBU

COLOUR RATING
7.8 EBC

FOR THE MASH

LIQUOR 11.5 litres (20 pints) **MASH TIME** 1 hr **TEMPERATURE** 65°C (149°F)

Grain bill	Quantity
Wheat malt	2.3kg (5lb)
Pale malt	2.3kg (5lb)

FOR THE BOIL

LIQUOR 27 litres (47½ pints) **BOIL TIME** 1 hr 10 mins

Hops	Quantity	IBU	When to add
Saaz 4.2%	32g (1oz)	15.3	At start of boil

Other			
Protofloc	1 tsp		For last 15 mins of boil
Curaçao bitter orange peel	25g (1oz)		For last 10 mins of boil
Coriander seeds, lightly crushed	25g (1oz)		For last 10 mins of boil

TO FERMENT

FERMENTATION 24°C (75°F) **CONDITIONING** 3 weeks at 12°C (54°F)

Yeast
Wyeast 3944 Belgian witbier

BREWER'S TIP

Ensure you have plenty of space at the top of the fermenter as this yeast creates a huge head during fermentation.

MALT EXTRACT VERSION

Add 2.7kg (6lb) **dried wheat malt extract** to 27 litres (47½ pints) of water, bring to a boil, and add the hops and other ingredients as specified in the main recipe.

QUICK BREW

This moreish, creamy, German wheat beer has a complex malt character that fuses well with the mix of fruity flavours imparted by the blended yeast strain.

QUICK BREW

Dunkelweizen

ORIGINAL GRAVITY 1056 **EXPECTED FINAL GRAVITY** 1014 **TOTAL LIQUOR** 32.5 LITRES (57 PINTS)

 MAKES 23 LITRES (40 PINTS)

 READY TO DRINK 4 WEEKS

 ESTIMATED ABV 5.6%

 BITTERNESS RATING 15.3 IBU

 COLOUR RATING 29.5 EBC

FOR THE MASH

LIQUOR 13.5 litres (23¾ pints) **MASH TIME** 1 hr **TEMPERATURE** 65°C (149°F)

Grain bill	Quantity
Wheat malt	2.7kg (6lb)
Munich malt	2.3kg (5lb)
Caramunich III	300g (10½oz)
Special B	300g (10½oz)

FOR THE BOIL

LIQUOR 27 litres (47½ pints) **BOIL TIME** 1 hr 10 mins

Hops	Quantity	IBU	When to add
Tettnang 4.5%	32g (1oz)	15.3	At start of boil

Other			
Protofloc	1 tsp		For last 15 mins of boil

TO FERMENT

FERMENTATION 22°C (72°F) **CONDITIONING** 3 weeks at 12°C (54°F)

Yeast
Wyeast 3056 Bavarian wheat

More like an ale than a traditional wheat beer, this dark and malty brew has the distinct flavour and character of wheat but with a hoppy, citrus aroma and flavour.

Dark Wheat Beer

ORIGINAL GRAVITY 1064 **EXPECTED FINAL GRAVITY** 1015 **TOTAL LIQUOR** 33.5 LITRES (59 PINTS)

 MAKES 23 LITRES (40 PINTS)

 READY TO DRINK 6 WEEKS

 ESTIMATED ABV 6.5%

 BITTERNESS RATING 44 IBU

 COLOUR RATING 28.8 EBC

FOR THE MASH

LIQUOR 16.25 litres (28½ pints) **MASH TIME** 1 hr **TEMPERATURE** 65°C (149°F)

Grain bill	Quantity
Vienna malt	3kg (6lb 10oz)
Wheat malt	2.6kg (5lb 12oz)
Biscuit malt	500g (1lb 2oz)
Crystal wheat	300g (10½oz)
Carafa special I	100g (3½oz)

FOR THE BOIL

LIQUOR 27 litres (47½ pints) **BOIL TIME** 1 hr 10 mins

Hops	Quantity	IBU	When to add
Magnum 11%	40g (1⅓oz)	44.1	At start of boil
Willamette 6.3%	24g (¾oz)	0.0	At turn off

Other			
Protofloc	1 tsp		For last 15 mins of boil

TO FERMENT

FERMENTATION 18°C (64°F) **CONDITIONING** 5 weeks at 12°C (54°F)

Yeast
Wyeast 2565 Kölsch

Mixed styles

The beers in this category can't be neatly defined as a lager, ale, or wheat beer – although they may share certain qualities and brewing techniques.

Included in this group are hybrid beers, which often use a combination of lager and ale fermentation methods. Kölsch (see p197), for example, is brewed as an ale with top-fermenting yeast but is conditioned in cool conditions and has a clean, lager finish. Californian Common (see p198), on the other hand, is produced with lager yeast but is fermented at warmer ale temperatures.

GET CREATIVE
For the creative home brewer, herb, spice, fruit, and even vegetable beers are perfect for experimentation. Use the recipes in this section as a starting point from which to build your own repertoire of wild and wonderful brews. As long as you pick complementary flavours and use appropriate quantities, there's no reason why you can't produce an exciting and delicious beer from any number of natural ingredients.

THREE KEYS TO SUCCESS
■ Add fruit to the fermenter after primary fermentation is complete – when the presence of alcohol will reduce the chance of bacterial infection – rather than to the boiler, as a lot of the fruit character will be lost if the fruit is boiled.

■ Add herbs and spices to the boil to allow them to infuse, but only for a few minutes at the end. If boiled for too long, the delicate flavours and aromas will be cooked away and replaced by bitter, or even astringent, characteristics. Herbs and spices can also be added directly to the fermenter after primary fermentation is complete.

■ Less is more when it comes to quantities – a subtle herb, spice, fruit, or vegetable character is usually more desirable than an overly assertive flavour.

Light hybrids

These beers use bottom-fermenting lager yeasts but are fermented at ale temperatures to create a full-bodied ale flavour with a clean lager finish.

● **Appearance** Depends on the style, but often very pale, crystal clear, and with a persistent white head.

● **Taste** Depends on the style, but usually clean with low bitterness and a dry finish.

(ψψψ) **Aroma** Typically neutral aroma with a low malt and hop presence.

▯ **Strength** 3.8–5.6% ABV

(US) Cream ales are popular American hybrid beers. They are light, clean, and very refreshing.

(DE) Kölsch is light, hoppy, clear, and brewed using top-fermenting yeast. The name is protected and restricted to about 20 breweries in and around Cologne, Germany.

▮ See pp196–97

Amber hybrids

Similar to light hybrids, but brewed with roasted malts for greater depth of flavour, these light brown beers are also known as bitter-lagers.

- **Appearance** Light brown to deep copper, usually very clear with good head retention.
- **Taste** Fairly bitter and malty, with a clean, crisp finish.
- **Aroma** Moderately hoppy with subtle malt aromas, depending on the style.
- **Strength** 4.5–5.5% ABV
- (DE) Altbiers from northern Germany – and Düsseldorf in particular – are typical amber hybrids. The name ("old beer") refers to the traditional brewing process in which ale yeast is fermented at cool, lager temperatures.

📖 **See pp198–201**

Herb and spice beers

Use only small amounts of herbs and spices when experimenting with different flavours.

- **Appearance** Usually clear, with the colour varying greatly, depending on the nature of the ingredients.
- **Taste** Generally dry with a subtle character from the herbs and spices.
- **Aroma** Can have a mild hoppiness, although the herbs will provide the dominant aroma.
- **Strength** 4–6% ABV
- (GB) Fraoch, meaning "heather" in Gaelic, is an ancient and unique style that has been brewed in Scotland for thousands of years.

📖 **See pp202–5**

Fruit and vegetable beers

Fruit and vegetables impart depth of flavour and add great character to a beer.

- **Appearance** Depends on the fruit or vegetables used, but often slightly hazy.
- **Taste** The particular fruit or vegetables added will provide the dominant flavours, although this should be subtle and balanced by hop bitterness.
- **Aroma** A light hop and malt aroma should perfectly complement the fruit or vegetable character.
- **Strength** 4–6% ABV
- (BE) Fruit wheat beers and cherry lambics are popular Belgian styles. Peach and raspberry beers are also common.
- (US) Pumpkin beer is an autumn favourite in the US; pale ale brewed with chilli pepper is also popular.

📖 **See pp206–11**

A classic American ale, this beer is light, crisp, and very refreshing on a warm summer's day. The subtle citrus aromas are perfectly balanced by a clean, neutral finish.

QUICK BREW

Cream Ale

ORIGINAL GRAVITY 1055   **EXPECTED FINAL GRAVITY** 1014   **TOTAL LIQUOR** 32.5 LITRES (57 PINTS)

 MAKES
23 LITRES
(40 PINTS)

 READY TO DRINK
4 WEEKS

 ESTIMATED ABV
5.5%

 BITTERNESS RATING
19.8 IBU

 COLOUR RATING
9.6 EBC

FOR THE MASH
LIQUOR 13.75 litres (24¼ pints)   **MASH TIME** 1 hr   **TEMPERATURE** 65°C (149°F)

Grain bill	Quantity
Pale malt	5kg (11lb)
Flaked maize	500g (1lb 2oz)

FOR THE BOIL
LIQUOR 27 litres (47½ pints)   **BOIL TIME** 1 hr 10 mins

Hops	Quantity	IBU	When to add
Centennial 8.5%	22g (¾oz)	19.8	At start of boil
Mount Hood 4.5%	33g (1¼oz)	0.0	At turn off

Other			
Protofloc	1 tsp		For last 15 mins of boil

TO FERMENT
FERMENTATION 18°C (64°F)
CONDITIONING 3 weeks at 12°C (54°F)

Yeast
Wyeast 2112 California lager

A German speciality brew, Kölsch is top-fermented like an ale but conditioned at low temperatures like a lager. It has a subtle, floral hoppiness and a clean character.

QUICK BREW

Kölsch

ORIGINAL GRAVITY 1046 **EXPECTED FINAL GRAVITY** 1011 **TOTAL LIQUOR** 31.5 LITRES (55½ PINTS)

MAKES
23 LITRES
(40 PINTS)

READY TO DRINK
4 WEEKS

ESTIMATED ABV
4.6%

BITTERNESS RATING
25 IBU

COLOUR RATING
7.2 EBC

FOR THE MASH

LIQUOR 11.25 litres (20 pints) **MASH TIME** 1 hr **TEMPERATURE** 65°C (149°F)

Grain bill	Quantity
Pilsner malt	4kg (8lb 13oz)
Carapils malt	500g (1lb 2oz)

FOR THE BOIL

LIQUOR 27 litres (47½ pints) **BOIL TIME** 1 hr 10 mins

Hops	Quantity	IBU	When to add
Spalt Select 4.5%	44g (1½oz)	22.8	At start of boil
Tettnang 4.5%	22g (¾oz)	2.2	For last 5 mins of boil
Tettnang 4.5%	44g (1½oz)	0.0	At turn off

Other			
Protofloc	1 tsp		For last 15 mins of boil

TO FERMENT

FERMENTATION 18°C (64°F) **CONDITIONING** 3 weeks at 12°C (54°F)

Yeast
Wyeast 2565 Kölsch

MALT EXTRACT VERSION

Steep 500g (1lb 2oz) **Carapils malt** in 27 litres (47½ pints) of water at 65°C (149°F) for 30 mins. Remove the malt, then add 2.5kg (5½lb) **dried extra light malt extract**, bring to a boil, and add the hops as specified in the main recipe.

This is an American-style amber ale with a clean, lager-like finish. The woody, minty hop aromas and flavours come from the German Northern Brewer hops.

Californian Common

ORIGINAL GRAVITY 1052 **EXPECTED FINAL GRAVITY** 1016 **TOTAL LIQUOR** 32 LITRES (56 PINTS)

 MAKES
23 LITRES
(40 PINTS)

 READY TO DRINK
6 WEEKS

 ESTIMATED ABV
4.8%

 BITTERNESS RATING
40.5 IBU

 COLOUR RATING
21.8 EBC

FOR THE MASH

LIQUOR 13 litres (23 pints) **MASH TIME** 1 hr **TEMPERATURE** 65°C (149°F)

Grain bill	Quantity
Pale malt	3.8kg (8lb 6oz)
Vienna malt	1kg (2¼lb)
Crystal malt	300g (10½oz)
Chocolate malt	50g (1¾oz)

FOR THE BOIL

LIQUOR 27 litres (47½ pints) **BOIL TIME** 1 hr 10 mins

Hops	Quantity	IBU	When to add
Northern Brewer 8%	41g (1½oz)	36.3	At start of boil
Northern Brewer 8%	14g (½oz)	4.2	For last 10 mins of boil
Northern Brewer 8%	41g (1½oz)	0.0	At turn off
Other			
Protofloc	1 tsp		For last 15 mins of boil

TO FERMENT

FERMENTATION 18°C (64°F) **CONDITIONING** 5 weeks at 12°C (54°F)

Yeast
Wyeast 2112 California lager

This is a fine example of a typical altbier, or "old beer", from Germany. It is a clean, dark brown, relatively bitter beer with a caramelly maltiness.

North German Altbier

ORIGINAL GRAVITY 1048 EXPECTED FINAL GRAVITY 1012 TOTAL LIQUOR 32 LITRES (56 PINTS)

 MAKES 23 LITRES (40 PINTS)   **READY TO DRINK** 8 WEEKS   **ESTIMATED ABV** 4.8%   **BITTERNESS RATING** 34.9 IBU   **COLOUR RATING** 26.5 EBC

FOR THE MASH

LIQUOR 13 litres (23 pints) **MASH TIME** 1 hr **TEMPERATURE** 65°C (149°F)

Grain bill	Quantity
Pilsner malt	2kg (4½lb)
Pale malt	2kg (4½lb)
Caramunich III	500g (1lb 2oz)
Carapils	300g (10½oz)
Carafa special III	60g (2oz)

FOR THE BOIL

LIQUOR 27 litres (47½ pints) **BOIL TIME** 1 hr 10 mins

Hops	Quantity	IBU	When to add
Magnum 11%	28g (1oz)	34.7	At start of boil
Other			
Protofloc	1 tsp		For last 15 mins of boil

TO FERMENT

FERMENTATION 12°C (54°F) **CONDITIONING** 7 weeks at 3°C (37°F)

Yeast
Wyeast 1007 German ale

MALT EXTRACT VERSION

Steep 500g (1lb 2oz) **Caramunich III**, 300g (10½oz) **Carapils malt**, and 60g (2oz) **Carafa special III** in 27 litres (47½ pints) of water at 65°C (149°F) for 30 mins. Remove the malt, then add 2.5kg (5½lb) **dried extra light malt extract**, bring to a boil, and add the hops as specified in the main recipe.

Düsseldorf Altbier is stronger and more bitter than altbiers brewed in other areas. Cool fermentation and extended lagering produce a smooth, silky ale.

Düsseldorf Altbier

ORIGINAL GRAVITY 1053 **EXPECTED FINAL GRAVITY** 1013 **TOTAL LIQUOR** 32 LITRES (56 PINTS)

 MAKES 23 LITRES (40 PINTS)

 READY TO DRINK 8 WEEKS

 ESTIMATED ABV 5.3%

 BITTERNESS RATING 49.6 IBU

COLOUR RATING 22.1 EBC

FOR THE MASH

LIQUOR 13 litres (23 pints) **MASH TIME** 1 hr **TEMPERATURE** 65°C (149°F)

Grain bill	Quantity
Pilsner malt	4.8kg (10lb 9oz)
Light crystal	350g (12oz)
Black malt	70g (2½oz)

FOR THE BOIL

LIQUOR 27 litres (47½ pints) **BOIL TIME** 1 hr 10 mins

Hops	Quantity	IBU	When to add
Spalt Select 4.5%	93g (3¼oz)	45.3	At start of boil
Spalt Select 4.5 %	46g (1½oz)	4.4	For last 5 mins of boil
Spalt Select 4.5%	50g (1¾oz)	0.0	At turn off
Other			
Protofloc	1 tsp		For last 15 mins of boil

TO FERMENT

FERMENTATION 18°C (64°F) **CONDITIONING** 7 weeks at 3°C (37°F)

Yeast
Wyeast 1275 Thames Valley ale

MALT EXTRACT VERSION

Steep 350g (12oz) **light crystal malt** and 70g (2½oz) **black malt** in 27 litres (47½ pints) of water at 65°C (149°F) for 30 mins. Remove the malt, then add 3kg (6lb 10oz) **dried extra light malt extract**, bring to a boil, and add the hops as specified in the main recipe.

The flavours in this unusual beer work surprisingly well together. With notes of spice and citrus, and a hoppy aroma, it is a great beer to enjoy with spicy food.

Spiced Coriander and Lime Beer

ORIGINAL GRAVITY 1050 **EXPECTED FINAL GRAVITY** 1011 **TOTAL LIQUOR** 32 LITRES (56 PINTS)

 MAKES 23 LITRES (40 PINTS)

 READY TO DRINK 4 WEEKS

 ESTIMATED ABV 5.1%

 BITTERNESS RATING 37.1 IBU

 COLOUR RATING 9 EBC

FOR THE MASH
LIQUOR 12.5 litres (22 pints) **MASH TIME** 1 hr **TEMPERATURE** 65°C (149°F)

Grain bill	Quantity
Pale malt	4kg (8lb 13oz)
Carapils	500g (1lb 2oz)
Wheat malt	500g (1lb 2oz)

FOR THE BOIL
LIQUOR 27 litres (47½ pints) **BOIL TIME** 1 hr 10 mins

Hops	Quantity	IBU	When to add
Magnum 16%	20g (⅔oz)	35.4	At start of boil
Liberty 4.5%	10g (⅓oz)	1.7	For last 10 mins of boil
Liberty 4.5%	30g (1oz)	0.0	At turn off

Other			
Protofloc	1 tsp		For last 15 mins of boil
Coriander seeds, crushed	25g (1oz)		For last 10 mins of boil

TO FERMENT
FERMENTATION 18°C (64°F) **CONDITIONING** 2 weeks at 12°C (54°F)

Yeast
Whitelabs WLP001 California ale

Hops/other	Quantity	When to add
Styrian Golding Bobek	50g (1¾oz)	After 4 days, leave for about 1 week
Dried lemongrass, crushed	4 stalks	As above
Dried kaffir lime leaves	5g (¼oz)	As above
Fresh ginger, grated	50g (1¾oz)	As above

Traditionally brewed using only spruce tips and molasses, this modern version retains the resinous character of the spruce but results in a more well-rounded ale.

Spruce Beer

ORIGINAL GRAVITY 1051 **EXPECTED FINAL GRAVITY** 1014 **TOTAL LIQUOR** 32 LITRES (56 PINTS)

 MAKES 23 LITRES (40 PINTS)   **READY TO DRINK** 6 WEEKS   **ESTIMATED ABV** 4.8%   **BITTERNESS RATING** 25 IBU   **COLOUR RATING** 15.5 EBC

FOR THE MASH

LIQUOR 12.75 litres (22⅓ pints) **MASH TIME** 1 hr **TEMPERATURE** 65°C (149°F)

Grain bill	Quantity
Pale malt	4.4kg (9lb 11oz)
Caramalt	500g (1lb 2oz)
Crystal wheat	200g (7oz)

FOR THE BOIL

LIQUOR 27 litres (47½ pints) **BOIL TIME** 1 hr 10 mins

Hops	Quantity	IBU	When to add
Magnum 16%	14g (½oz)	25.0	At start of boil
Magnum 16%	7g (¼oz)	0.0	At turn off

Other			
Spruce tips	150g (5½oz)		At start of boil
Protofloc	1 tsp		For last 15 mins of boil

TO FERMENT

FERMENTATION 18°C (64°F) **CONDITIONING** 4 weeks at 12°C (54°F)

Yeast
Whitelabs WLP013 London ale

Hops	Quantity	When to add
Apollo 19.5%	50g (1¾oz)	After 4 days, leave for about 1 week

This cloudy, spicy brew is similar to a Belgian wheat beer but has a dry, honey finish. Clove, orange, and spicy coriander flavours make this a unique and refreshing beer.

QUICK BREW

Spiced Honey Beer

ORIGINAL GRAVITY 1051 **EXPECTED FINAL GRAVITY** 1009 **TOTAL LIQUOR** 32 LITRES (56 PINTS)

 MAKES 23 LITRES (40 PINTS)

 READY TO DRINK 4 WEEKS

 ESTIMATED ABV 5.6%

 BITTERNESS RATING 11.6 IBU

 **COLOUR RATING** 9.1 EBC

FOR THE MASH

LIQUOR 11 litres (19½ pints) **MASH TIME** 1 hr **TEMPERATURE** 65°C (149°F)

Grain bill	Quantity
Pale malt	4.4kg (9lb 11oz)

FOR THE BOIL

LIQUOR 27 litres (47½ pints) **BOIL TIME** 1 hr 10 mins

Hops	Quantity	IBU	When to add
Hallertauer Hersbrucker 4.1%	22g (¾oz)	10.6	At start of boil
Hallertauer Hersbrucker 4.1%	5g (¼oz)	0.9	For last 5 mins of boil
Hallertauer Hersbrucker 4.1%	6g (¼oz)	0.1	For last 1 min of boil

Other			
Protofloc	1 tsp		For last 15 mins of boil
Coriander seeds, crushed	38g (1¼oz)		For last 10 mins of boil
Curaçao bitter orange peel	16g (½oz)		For last 10 mins of boil
Honey	500g (1lb 2oz)		For last 10 mins of boil

TO FERMENT

FERMENTATION 24°C (75°F) **CONDITIONING** 3 weeks at 12°C (54°F)

Yeast
Wyeast 3068 Weihenstephan Weizen

MALT EXTRACT VERSION

Add 2.7kg (6lb) **dried extra light malt extract** to 27 litres (47½ pints) of water, bring to a boil, and add the hops as specified in the main recipe.

This brew is more like an ale with added ginger than a traditional ginger beer. Its distinct spicy character is complemented by the citrus qualities of the Galaxy hops.

Ginger Beer

ORIGINAL GRAVITY 1045 **EXPECTED FINAL GRAVITY** 1011 **TOTAL LIQUOR** 32.5 LITRES (57 PINTS)

 MAKES 23 LITRES (40 PINTS)   **READY TO DRINK** 4 WEEKS   **ESTIMATED ABV** 4.5%   **BITTERNESS RATING** 25.1 IBU   **COLOUR RATING** 6.3 EBC

FOR THE MASH

LIQUOR 13.75 litres (24¼ pints) **MASH TIME** 1 hr **TEMPERATURE** 65°C (149°F)

Grain bill	Quantity
Lager malt	3.5kg (7lb 11oz)
Flaked maize	1kg (2¼lb)

FOR THE BOIL

LIQUOR 27 litres (47½ pints) **BOIL TIME** 1 hr 10 mins

Hops	Quantity	IBU	When to add
Galaxy 14.4%	14g (½oz)	22.9	At start of boil
Galaxy 14.4%	7g (¼oz)	2.1	For last 5 mins of boil
Galaxy 14.4%	20g (⅔oz)	0.0	At turn off

Other			
Protofloc	1 tsp		For last 15 mins of boil
Freshly grated ginger	150g (5½oz)		For last 5 mins of boil

TO FERMENT

FERMENTATION 18°C (64°F) **CONDITIONING** 3 weeks at 12°C (54°F)

Yeast
Wyeast 1028 London ale

BREWER'S TIP

To give the finished beer a really intense, fiery flavour, add more freshly grated ginger – up to 300g (10½oz) – to the boil.

Adding raspberries during fermentation makes this Belgian-style wheat beer simply irresistible. It's a great summer brew that is sure to convert non-beer drinkers!

QUICK BREW

Raspberry Wheat Beer

ORIGINAL GRAVITY 1050 EXPECTED FINAL GRAVITY 1012 TOTAL LIQUOR 32 LITRES (56 PINTS)

 MAKES 23 LITRES (40 PINTS)   **READY TO DRINK** 4 WEEKS   **ESTIMATED ABV** 5.1%   **BITTERNESS RATING** 15.3 IBU   **COLOUR RATING** 7.2 EBC

FOR THE MASH

LIQUOR 12.5 litres (22 pints) MASH TIME 1 hr TEMPERATURE 65°C (149°F)

Grain bill	Quantity
Lager malt	2.7kg (6lb)
Wheat malt	2.3kg (5lb)

FOR THE BOIL

LIQUOR 27 litres (47½ pints) BOIL TIME 1 hr 10 mins

Hops	Quantity	IBU	When to add
Challenger 7%	20g (⅔oz)	15.0	At start of boil

Other			
Protofloc	1 tsp		For last 15 mins of boil

TO FERMENT

FERMENTATION 22°C (72°F) CONDITIONING 2 weeks at 12°C (54°F)

Yeast
Wyeast 1010 American wheat

Other	Quantity	When to add
Raspberries	2.5kg (5½lb)	After 2 days, leave for about 1 week

BREWER'S TIP

Substitute frozen raspberries for the fresh ones if you prefer – they work just as well and are often less expensive.

MALT EXTRACT VERSION

Add 3kg (6lb 10oz) **dried light malt extract** to 27 litres (47½ pints) of water, bring to a boil, and add the hops as specified in the main recipe.

The fresh fruit in this delicious and refreshing summer beer adds a subtle, dry strawberry flavour that is not as sweet or overpowering as you might expect.

QUICK
BREW

Strawberry Beer

ORIGINAL GRAVITY 1044 **EXPECTED FINAL GRAVITY** 1010 **TOTAL LIQUOR** 33 LITRES (58 PINTS)

 MAKES
23 LITRES
(40 PINTS)

 READY TO DRINK
4 WEEKS

 ESTIMATED ABV
4.4%

 BITTERNESS RATING
18.4 IBU

COLOUR RATING
8 EBC

FOR THE MASH

LIQUOR 14.5 litres (25½ pints) **MASH TIME** 1 hr **TEMPERATURE** 65°C (149°F)

Grain bill	Quantity
Lager malt	3.4kg (7½lb)
Munich malt	750g (1lb 10oz)
Torrified wheat malt	250g (9oz)

FOR THE BOIL

LIQUOR 27 litres (47½ pints) **BOIL TIME** 1 hr 10 mins

Hops	Quantity	IBU	When to add
Challenger 7%	20g (⅔oz)	16.2	At start of boil
Styrian Golding Celeia 5.5%	10g (⅓oz)	2.2	For last 10 mins of boil
Styrian Golding Celeia 5.5%	30g (1oz)	0.0	At turn off

Other			
Protofloc	1 tsp		For last 15 mins of boil

TO FERMENT

FERMENTATION 18°C (64°F) **CONDITIONING** 2 weeks at 12°C (54°F)

Yeast
Whitelabs WLP001 California ale

Other	Quantity	When to add
Strawberries	3.5kg (7lb 11oz)	After 4 days, leave for about 1 week

The kiwi fruit in this New Zealand-style witbier lends citrus notes to the brew and gives it a striking twist. The complex fruit flavours are unusual yet satisfying.

Kiwi Wheat Beer

ORIGINAL GRAVITY 1055 **EXPECTED FINAL GRAVITY** 1013 **TOTAL LIQUOR** 32.5 LITRES (57 PINTS)

 MAKES
23 LITRES
(40 PINTS)

 READY TO DRINK
6 WEEKS

 ESTIMATED ABV
5.5%

 BITTERNESS RATING
22.4 IBU

 COLOUR RATING
7.7 EBC

FOR THE MASH
LIQUOR 13.75 litres (24¼ pints) **MASH TIME** 1 hr **TEMPERATURE** 65°C (149°F)

Grain bill	Quantity
Lager malt	3kg (6lb 10oz)
Wheat malt	2.5kg (5½lb)

FOR THE BOIL
LIQUOR 27 litres (47½ pints) **BOIL TIME** 1 hr 10 mins

Hops	Quantity	IBU	When to add
Challenger 7%	30g (1oz)	22.4	At start of boil
Styrian Golding Celeia 5.5%	20g (⅔oz)	0.0	At turn off

Other	Quantity		When to add
Protofloc	1 tsp		For last 15 mins of boil
Coriander seeds, crushed	25g (1oz)		For last 5 mins of boil

TO FERMENT
FERMENTATION 22°C (72°F) **CONDITIONING** 4 weeks at 12°C (54°F)

Yeast
Wyeast 3463 forbidden fruit

Other	Quantity	When to add
Kiwi fruit, peeled and chopped	1.5kg (3lb 3oz)	After 4 days, leave for about 1 week

MALT EXTRACT VERSION
Add 2.8kg (6lb 3oz) **dried light malt extract** to 27 litres (47½ pints) of water, bring to a boil, and add the hops and other ingredients as specified in the main recipe.

MIXED STYLES FRUIT AND VEGETABLE BEERS

Traditionally brewed in colonial America as a cheap, local alternative to malt beers, this seasonal ale is subtly spiced to complement the distinct pumpkin character.

Pumpkin Ale

ORIGINAL GRAVITY 1050 **EXPECTED FINAL GRAVITY** 1012 **TOTAL LIQUOR** 32 LITRES (56 PINTS)

 MAKES
23 LITRES
(40 PINTS)

 READY TO DRINK
6 WEEKS

 ESTIMATED ABV
5.2%

BITTERNESS RATING
22.8 IBU

COLOUR RATING
15.7 EBC

FOR THE MASH

LIQUOR 12.5 litres (22 pints) **MASH TIME** 1 hr **TEMPERATURE** 65°C (149°F)

Grain bill	Quantity
Pale malt	3.4kg (7½lb)
Munich malt	1kg (2¼lb)
Wheat malt	500g (1lb 2oz)
Special B	100g (3½oz)

1 large pumpkin, roasted for 1 hr, then cut into cubes and added to the mash with the grains

FOR THE BOIL

LIQUOR 27 litres (47½ pints) **BOIL TIME** 1 hr 10 mins

Hops	Quantity	IBU	When to add
Magnum 16%	12g (½oz)	21.8	At start of boil
Hallertauer Mittelfrüh 5%	9g (⅓oz)	1.0	For last 5 mins of boil

Other			
Protofloc	1 tsp		For last 15 mins of boil
Cinnamon stick	1 stick		For last 5 mins of boil
Ground ginger	½ tsp		For last 5 mins of boil
Vanilla pod	2cm (¾in) piece		For last 5 mins of boil
Whole cloves, crushed	2 cloves		For last 5 mins of boil

TO FERMENT

FERMENTATION 18°C (64°F) **CONDITIONING** 5 weeks at 12°C (54°F)

Yeast
Whitelabs WLP001 California ale

QUICK BREW

Before the use of hops, nettles were used to flavour beer. This brew has the best of both worlds – an earthy spiciness from the nettles and floral, citrus notes from the hops.

Nettle Beer

ORIGINAL GRAVITY 1041 **EXPECTED FINAL GRAVITY** 1010 **TOTAL LIQUOR** 31 LITRES (54½ PINTS)

 MAKES 23 LITRES (40 PINTS)

 READY TO DRINK 4 WEEKS

 ESTIMATED ABV 4%

 BITTERNESS RATING 25 IBU

 COLOUR RATING 9.3 EBC

FOR THE MASH

LIQUOR 10 litres (17½ pints) **MASH TIME** 1 hr **TEMPERATURE** 65°C (149°F)

Grain bill	Quantity
Pale malt	3kg (6lb 10oz)
Munich malt	1kg (2¼lb)

FOR THE BOIL

LIQUOR 27 litres (47½ pints) **BOIL TIME** 1 hr 10 mins

Hops	Quantity	IBU	When to add
Fuggle 4.5%	38g (1¼oz)	20.1	At start of boil
Willamette 6.3%	19g (⅔oz)	4.9	For last 10 mins of boil
Styrian Golding Celeia 5.5%	19g (⅔oz)	0.0	At turn off

Other			
Freshly picked nettle tops	100g (3½oz)		At start of boil
Protofloc	1 tsp		For last 15 mins of boil

TO FERMENT

FERMENTATION 18°C (64°F)
CONDITIONING 3 weeks at 12°C (54°F)

Yeast
Wyeast 1275 Thames Valley ale

Useful information

FREQUENTLY ASKED QUESTIONS

1) How can I increase the alcohol content of my beer?

The simple answer is: add more sugar. During fermentation, the yeast will ferment this additional sugar and produce additional alcohol as a by-product. It is best to use dried malt extract (DME) as your sugar source, as it will introduce additional alcohol without increasing the overall sweetness of the beer. It is important to bear in mind that the yeast will only be able to effectively ferment a certain amount of additional DME or sugar, so follow these guidelines for a 23-litre (40-pint) batch:

- 500g (1lb 2oz) DME will increase the ABV by approximately 0.5%
- 1kg (2¼lb) DME will increase the ABV by approximately 1%
- 500g (1lb 2oz) brown sugar will increase the ABV by approximately 0.9%
- 500g (1lb 2oz) maple syrup will increase the ABV by approximately 0.7%
- 1kg (1lb 2oz) honey will increase the ABV by approximately 0.7%

2) Why is the original gravity (OG) lower than expected?

There are three likely causes for this:

- You have added too much water to a kit or malt-extract recipe. With full-mash recipes, a low OG may indicate that the mash efficiency is low.
- You have not stirred the wort properly after adding water to a kit or malt-extract receipe. This will leave all the sugars at the bottom of the fermenter, causing the gravity to be too low at the top.
- The pre-fermented wort was too cool or too hot when you took a gravity reading. Hydrometers are calibrated to take readings when the wort is at a set temperature – typically 20°C (68°F) – so if it is cooler or hotter than this, the results will be inaccurate.

3) How long will my beer keep for?

As long as the beer does not become oxidized once it has been bottled or barreled, it should keep for several months. In fact, many styles will benefit from extended ageing.

4) How do I know if my beer has started to ferment?

A thick foam should form on top – usually within 24 hours of the yeast being pitched. This is completely normal and actually protects the beer during fermentation. The best way to check how fermentation is progressing is to take a hydrometer reading and see if it is lower than the original gravity. If your beer hasn't started fermenting after 48 hours, check that it is at the correct temperature and adjust if necessary. If the temperature is correct, then you will need to pitch more yeast.

5) Why is my beer flat?

Flat beer is caused by either too little priming sugar being added prior to bottling or barreling, or because the priming sugar has not been able to ferment due to the storage temperature being incorrect. If you are storing your beer in a barrel, try adding carbon dioxide. If the beer is still flat, check for leaks around the cap.

CONVERSION CHART

Volume

The recipes in this book make approximately:
23 litres / 40 pints (imperial) / 48 pints (US)
5 gallons (imperial) / 6 gallons (US)

To convert:

Litres to fluid ounces (imperial):	multiply by 35.195
Litres to cups (US):	multiply by 4.227
Litres to pints (imperial):	multiply by 1.76
Litres to pints (US):	multiply by 2.11
Litres to gallons (imperial):	multiply by 0.22
Litres to gallons (US):	multiply by 0.26

(To convert the other way, divide by the figures shown)

Weight

To convert:

Grams to ounces:	multiply by 0.035
Kilograms to pounds:	multiply by 2.205

(To convert the other way, divide by the figures shown)

Temperature

To convert:

°C to °F:	multiply by 1.8, then add 32
°F to °C:	subtract 32, then divide by 1.8

ONLINE FORUMS

www.jimsbeerkit.co.uk
A lively UK-based home-brewing forum, with lots of resources and good advice.

www.brewuk.co.uk/forums
A very friendly UK-based brewing forum, well suited for beginners.

www.homebrewtalk.com
A popular and friendly US-based home-brewing forum.

www.aussiehomebrewer.com
The largest Australian-based home-brewing forum.

USEFUL WEBSITES

www.mrmalty.com
A useful brewing resource, especially for yeast substitutions and yeast-starter calculations.

www.brewersfriend.com
A useful resource with calculators, spreadsheets, and a recipe builder.

www.beersmith.com
Includes downloadable software plus lots of additional brewing information.

www.beeralchemyapp.com
A downloadable application that creates recipes and tracks your ingredient orders.

www.beerlabelizer.com
Provides a series of design templates that allow you to customize and create your own beer labels.

USEFUL INFORMATION

Glossary

Adjunct Any fermentable ingredient that doesn't rely on *enzymes* to produce sugars.

Aerate To introduce oxygen to a solution to aid fermentation.

Airlock A small valve-like device that allows carbon dioxide to escape from the fermenter, but prevents air from entering.

Alcohol by volume (ABV) Alcoholic strength measured as the percentage volume of alcohol per volume of beer.

Alcohol by weight (ABW) Alcoholic strength measured as the percentage weight of alcohol per volume of beer.

Ale Any beer produced using a top-fermenting yeast.

All-grain beer Any beer produced using crushed malted barley.

Alpha acid The source of a beer's bitterness; derived from hops during the boil.

Apparent attenuation The percentage of sugars that have been fermented during fermentation. It is equal to the *original gravity* minus the *final gravity* divided by the original gravity. Most beers have an apparent attenuation of 60–80%.

Attenuation The lowering of the *gravity* of the *wort* as the yeast turns the sugars into alcohol.

Body A measure of the fullness or mouthfeel of a beer.

Carbonation The process whereby carbon dioxide gas is dissolved into the beer.

Carboy A container used to ferment and store beer. Also known as a demijohn, it is usually made of glass.

Chill haze A haziness caused by proteins in the *wort* that forms during boiling and cooling and which is noticeable in the finished beer when chilled.

Closed fermentation Fermentation in a sealed container usually fitted with an *airlock*.

Copper A brewing term for the boiler; used for boiling the *wort* with the hops.

Cold break Proteins in the *wort* that stick together and fall out of suspension in the liquid when it is cooled quickly.

Decoction A method of *mashing* in which a part of the mash is removed and boiled separately before being returned to the tun to increase the temperature.

Diacetyl A by-product of fermentation that can produce buttery or butterscotch flavours and aromas.

Dry hopping The process of adding fresh hops to the fermenter a few days into fermentation.

European Brewery Convention (EBC) A measure of the darkness of malts and beers – the higher the number, the darker the colour.

Enzymes Protein-based catalysts that effect changes in the substances in which they are found.

Esters Fruit flavour compounds that are produced by yeast during fermentation.

Extract A soluble substance usually created from malted barley or *adjuncts*.

Fermentation lock See *airlock*.

Final gravity The *gravity* of the beer once fermentation is complete.

Finings Ingredients added to the beer that help remove proteins and yeast cells and enable it to clear faster.

Flocculation The clumping together and settling out of yeast cells during fermentation.

Germination The part of the malting process during which the seeds begin to sprout.

Gravity The density of a solution compared to water.

Green malt *Malt* that has been steeped and germinated prior to heating.

Grist The mix of crushed grains used for *mashing*.

Hop pellets Powdered hop cones compressed in pellet form.

Hot break proteins that coagulate and fall out of suspension during the boil.

Hydrometer A device used to measure *gravity*.

International Bitterness Units (IBU) The standard unit for measuring the concentration of *alpha acids* in hops.

Isinglass A gelatine-like substance added to beer as a fining agent.

Irish moss A type of *finings* that encourages proteins in the *wort* to drop out of suspension during boiling and cooling.

Krausen The thick foamy head that forms during the early stages of fermentation.

Lager Any beer produced using bottom-fermenting yeast and usually at low temperatures.

Lag time The period of yeast growth after *pitching* and before fermentation starts.

Lovibond A unit of colour measurement, commonly used before the introduction of *EBC* and *SRM*.

Malt A grain (usually barley) that has been steeped, germinated, and kiln-dried during *malting*.

Malt extract The sweet, sugary solution created during *mashing* in concentrated form.

Malting The process in which grains (usually barley) are turned into *malt*.

Maltose The sugar compound created during *mashing*, which is then consumed by the yeast during fermentation.

Mashing The process of steeping *malt* in hot water to allow the enzymatic breakdown of the grains into soluble, fermentable sugars.

Modification The degree to which a *malt* has been converted ready for *mashing*.

Original gravity The *gravity* of the *wort* before fermentation starts.

pH The unit used to measure the acidity or alkalinity of a solution on a scale of 1–14, where 1 is the most acidic and 14 the most alkaline.

Pitching The process of adding yeast to the *wort* in the fermenter to start *primary fermentation*.

Primary fermentation The most active stage of fermentation, when the yeast is converting sugars in the *wort* into alcohol and carbon dioxide.

Priming The process of adding sugar to the beer prior to bottling or kegging to add fizz. The sugar ferments, creating carbon dioxide that dissolves in the beer.

Protofloc A fining agent similar to *Irish moss*.

Racking The process of transferring liquid from one vessel to another.

Real ale Any beer that is served directly from the cask without the application of carbon dioxide.

Rousing Stirring or mixing; usually to stimulate yeast back into suspension.

Runnings The liquid produced during *mashing*.

Sparging The process of rinsing sugars from the grain after *mashing*.

Standard Reference Method (SRM) An alternative scale to *EBC*.

Starch The main form of energy storage for most plants.

Starter A small batch of fermenting yeast, normally created prior to *pitching*, which increases the overall number of yeast cells.

Sterilizing The process of killing unwanted bacteria.

Strike temperature The target temperature for *mashing*, once the water and grains have been mixed.

Tannin Astringent compounds usually found in grain husks and hop-cone material.

Trub The layer of sediment that forms at the bottom of the fermenter, consisting mainly of protein and dead yeast cells.

Wort The name of the sugary solution, prior to *pitching*, that will ultimately become beer.

Index

INDEX

INDEX

223

About the author

Greg Hughes is an experienced home brewer, a leading member of the home-brewing industry, and co-owner and founder of BrewUK, one of the UK's largest online home-brewing retailers and community websites. He organizes national competitions in conjunction with some of the UK's leading commercial breweries, and encourages home brewers of all levels to improve their craft through continued support and product development. With a wealth of experience in all areas of home brewing, Greg specializes in the production of innumerable styles of ale.

Acknowledgments

The author would like to thank: A huge thank you to my wife, Tanya, and children, Rico and Macy. Without their support during all those long hours spent creating beers in the garage, this book would never have been possible.

DK would like to thank: Phil Robins at Longdog Brewery for checking the recipes; Tony Briscoe and Ian O'Leary for photography; Wei Tang for prop styling; Kate Fenton for design assistance; Chris Mooney and Elizabeth Clinton for editorial assistance; and Jane Bamforth for proofreading.

Picture credits: Page 14, bottom right: from a sixteenth-century woodcut by J. Ammon, previously published in *The Brewer's Art* by B. Meredith Brown.

All other images © Dorling Kindersley.
For further information see: **www.dkimages.com**

Warning: Please take care when following the instructions in this book, especially when boiling and transferring large quantities of liquids. The Publisher cannot accept responsibility for any accidents that may result from following the instructions contained in this book.